Life was meant to be
sipped not gulped.

Betsy Maly

SUPER NATURAL LIVING

SUPER NATURAL LIVING

Betty Malz

Published by

√chosen books

Lincoln, Virginia 22078

Library of Congress Cataloging in Publication Data

Malz, Betty.
    Super natural living.

    1. Christian life—1960-   2. Malz,
Betty.   I. Title.
BV4501.2.M335   248.4   82-1309
ISBN 0-912376-79-1   AACR2

This book is dedicated to:

Brenda, my pride
April, my joy
Connie, my love gift
and to Carl, my husband and inspiration.
(He tells me I can accomplish anything
that I attempt.)

ACKNOWLEDGEMENTS

Thanks to Sharon Perkins, my sister-in-law, for taking time from her own writing, to help with mine.

I appreciate Len LeSourd, my writing coach, for his professional advice which has been the blending agent that links my stories into readable book form.

CONTENTS

HOW IT ALL BEGAN

As I STARTED to write this book, my head ached and I felt chilled. *I'm coming down with the flu,* I thought. *And I'm lonely.*

My husband, Carl, had departed on a four-day business trip, leaving my daughter, April, and me alone in our big house. We live four miles from the nearest town on beautiful South Dakota farmland—but at that moment the ground outside was frozen and it was ten degrees below zero.

This particular morning our cat had been sick, the furnace kept shutting off, a mouse ran across the kitchen floor and April was late getting off to school. I wanted to go back to bed, not sit down to write.

The title of the book stared back at me from my papers. I had to laugh.

Super Natural Living! "Who can live like that?" I asked myself grumpily.

You can and should, came the quick answer from deep inside me.

I felt corrected. Then I did what I should have done several hours before—I prayed: "Lord, without You I'm a weak person, an insensitive wife and an inadequate mother. With You, nothing is impossible and living is an endless adventure."

Feeling better, I got down to work, aware that more obstacles than usual were being put in my way. But why? Was the subject *that* important?

Super Natural Living. Before he left on his trip, Carl spotted the title on the papers on top of my nightstand and stared hard at it for a moment.

"Oh, no!" he murmured.

"What's wrong?" I asked.

"That title!"

"You don't like it?"

"I *do* like it," he answered slowly. "But what will it do to us?"

"You sound fearful."

Carl stared at me for a long moment. "Our life is very intense as it is. This book will speed it up all the more."

I shook my head. "On the contrary, it may help us to slow down."

He looked at me in disbelief, then went to pack his bag.

For years the phrase "supernatural living" had been laid on my heart as something important. At first, I assumed it meant a kind of super piousness, elevated to a higher plane than most everyone else. Saintliness.

I looked up supernatural in the dictionary and read this definition: "Unexplainable by natural laws, superlative . . . characteristic of God." (God injects His "super" into my "natural.") It's like being mired down in one of our vehicles, stuck in forty-one inches of snow when we must reach out for power. So we shove that lever into *four-wheel drive*, the "baby" grinds and digs, then lurches powerfully forward, out, upward and *onward!*

Super natural living means superlative living. And its source is God, not man.

Soon I was off on a quest to find out more about what it really meant to live supernaturally. Strangely enough, the first clue came as I reviewed the story of my own birth....

1

IMPOSSIBLE SITUATION

Two young people in love had gone to the movie, *Sonny Boy*, starring Al Jolson. After the movie they drove to the girl's home in the young man's battered Ford Roadster. It was a warm summer night so they sat in the car talking, the song and the atmosphere of *Sonny Boy* lingering in their minds. Moonlight bathed the grape arbor on one side of the driveway, a cherry tree on the other.

Glenn Perkins, age twenty-three, and Fern Rosemond Burns, age eighteen, were making wedding plans. Though their parents wanted them to wait a few years, the two young people were determined to marry soon. They made another decision that night: their first child would be a son and they would name him "Sonny Boy." Fern voiced quite an ambition for a ninety-seven-pound slip of a girl, who played Jazz piano and tap-danced the "Charleston." "I want twelve children, a twelve-room house and a hundred acres of our own land," she sighed dreamily.

Impulsive young love had its way and Glenn and Fern were

married shortly thereafter. But the economic crash of 1929 that followed dampened their big dreams. Glenn lost his job. A baby was on the way, and the young couple was unable to pay the rent on their small house in Terre Haute, Indiana, or keep the place warm. And Fern was unable to keep any food down. It nearly crushed Glenn's pride when they had to move in with Fern's parents a few weeks before the baby was to be born.

But Glenn and Fern's troubles were only beginning. When labor pains started Tuesday evening, November 5, 1929, Fern was rushed to Union Hospital. The baby was only seven months along.

Everything had gone wrong that night as the doctor and nurses performed an emergency Caesarean section. At 6:45 the following morning when the doctor appeared, Glenn was almost paralyzed with fear. Dr. Ernest L. Mattox was still dressed in his surgical coat and his face was white with fatigue. Gently he placed a hand on the shoulder of the expectant father.

"It's been a long, hard battle and I'm afraid we're losing. The baby girl was stillborn, barely four pounds. We've put her in an incubator, but I'm afraid we can't save her. The mother is anemic, dangerously so. We don't have a good drug yet to cope with uremic poisoning and her inability to retain food weakened her and the baby. We're doing all we can."

Glenn Perkins was crushed by the news. Already suffering from a terrible migraine headache, he wandered dazed and heartbroken about the waiting room. Then Fern's great-uncle, Archie Brown, entered the room.

Something happened at that moment. Though few words were spoken, Glenn knew that help had arrived for suddenly his headache ceased. As he looked into the strong face of his friend, Glenn remembered that this man had returned from World War I as a walking miracle.

Archie Brown had been buried alive on the battle field under a mound of dirt during a shell explosion. His battalion gave up searching for him and were preparing to move away from enemy fire. Though Arch was not a religious man, at that moment he pleaded with God: "Help me, Lord. Make a way out. Let someone find me."

While equipment was being loaded, one man decided to shovel into one more mound of dirt before they withdrew. Was it coincidence that his shovel struck Arch Brown?

Arch had some lung damage, but recovered fully and came home with a ringing report of the miraculous power of God to hear prayer, to miraculously change the minds of men, and to heal.

He laid a hand on Glenn's shoulder — right where the doctor's hand had rested while he reported the death of the baby and the bad news about Fern — and quietly proclaimed good news. "Glenn, God will not fail you in this impossible situation." Uncle Arch quoted Hebrews 13:5: " 'I will never leave thee, nor forsake thee.' You can quote it backwards and it means the same, 'Thee forsake, nor thee leave, never will I!' So Satan cannot even twist it around or backward to cancel that promise!

"In the same chapter, verse eight, listen to these words: 'Jesus Christ the same yesterday, and today, and forever.' Some years ago, I experienced a miracle, today you will experience one if you can believe."

"If you can believe. If you can believe." The words echoed in Glenn's ears as he went outside in the fresh, November air to walk and to think.

Uncle Arch also went for a walk to Fern's room where the family waited sorrowfully for the end. Compassion gripped his heart as he looked at his grieving family. He walked to the hospital bed and laid his hand on Fern's fevered forehead; he was not daunted by her bluish appearance or her lifeless, anemic form, packed in ice bags. Softly, but firmly, he prayed, "Lord Jesus, our Great Physician, heal my niece, Fern."

Two things happened simultaneously. Fern Perkins blinked, opened her eyes and began to whisper, praying faintly with her lips barely moving. Then she pushed off the ice bags and sat up, amazing the doctor and her family.

In the nursery of the obstetrics ward the "lifeless" baby began to stir in the incubator that had been disconnected when her breathing seemed to have stopped. Nurse Helen Bauer quickly reconnected the incubator, then literally flew into the mother's room to shriek the startling news to Dr. Mattox who was still in a state of shock over what he himself had just witnessed with Fern Perkins.

Glenn Perkins then entered his wife's room, fearing what he would find. What he saw almost put him into shock! His wife was sitting up in bed, tears of joy running down her face, shouting "Our baby girl is alive . . . alive . . . alive!"

"Sonny Boy" was hardly the right name for a girl, so they named me Betty Eileen.

After several weeks in the hospital, my weight increased to five pounds. And after nutritious meals with high iron content, intravenous feedings and blood transfusions, my mother began to produce a nourishing, life-giving milk for me. We were both now ready to go home. The sun truly began to shine on our family.

Though the miracle of having his wife back had revolutionized Daddy's life, he did not understand the new dimension in my mother. In some ways it was almost as if he had lost her. Taking a Bible from the night stand in her hospital room, she read to him James 5:15: "And the prayer of faith shall save the sick."

Then my mother tried to help Daddy understand that she had become a new creature in Christ Jesus, old things had passed away and behold all things had become new (see II Corinthians 5:17), not just physically but supernaturally in the spiritual part of her being.

My father loved my mother so deeply that he wanted very much to understand. He was deeply grateful for the miraculous restoration of both his wife and daughter, but the strange aspects of all this frightened him. He didn't know that kind of God and wasn't sure he wanted to. Only the natural world was real to him. This other — well, it seemed unreal, yes, even spooky, for a man who earned a living working with his hands.

When the day came for Mother and me to leave the hospital, Daddy shook Dr. Mattox's hand with some anxiety. "I don't know when I'll ever be able to pay these hospital expenses. I have no job and am living with my in-laws. My father-in-law has had to close his grocery store and I'll be doing carpentry work with him for our board and room. But I'll send you something as often as I can. I don't suppose a busy doctor like you can understand this."

Laying his hand on my dad's shoulder the doctor replied, "Oh but I do understand. Only this morning I received a letter from my bank informing me that they were closing, that I may pick up only ten percent of my life's savings. Everyone is suffering. Few are paying for their medical services. Do the best you can."

We drove home from the hospital in my Aunt Lillian's car. My daddy was really "two people" sitting in the back seat holding his daughter for the first time. One part of him was jumping up and down with glee because his little family was intact: his wife now well and sitting beside him, their first production on his lap. The other half of him was tormented with worry. He had lost his car and felt degraded to have to sit in the back seat while Mother's sister drove us in her car. How was he to support his family?

Later that night Daddy asked his wife a question that had been on his mind for days. "Fern, what is it with Archie Brown?"

"What do you mean?"

"This power he has. I've seen him three times now. Each time I had a tension headache, and when he came into the room the headache vanished."

"The power is from God, dear. It has transformed him so

that he returned from death with a love for and a desire to
invest in people!"

Three nights later, after the 2:00 A.M. feeding, which Daddy
had watched with fascination, he slipped into the kitchen,
closed the door behind him, and dropped on his knees at the
kitchen chair. Slumping forward, mentally exhausted from
searching for answers for his life, he cried out, "Oh, God, if
there is a God, reveal Yourself to me." He shuddered with a
brief tinge of fear, for it seemed that heatless flames crackled
and licked all four of the walls about him, enveloping him and
the chair where he knelt.

Then suddenly it was over, and he knew a tranquil peace
akin to what he knew his wife had felt the day she prayed in
the hospital. He ran to the bedroom, knelt quickly on the
floor beside her sleeping form and, trembling, laid his head
upon her breast, awakening her. While she stroked his head,
he told her what had happened in the kitchen.

The following night they attended the church where Arch
Brown was pastor. Before the service was over, my dad was
kneeling at an old-fashioned altar, weeping out his uncertain-
ty, bitterness and past woe, in exchange for the new life which
had entered into him.

Then Dad got another surprise. He had fallen in love with
the *natural* dark-haired, blue-eyed beauty who could play
popular piano tunes and dance the latest steps. Now he met
the *supernatural* side of his young bride. Upon the invitation of
the pastor, Fern Perkins stepped to the piano and while ac-
companying herself, lifted the audience with these words:

> *"Lift me up above the shadows,*
> *lift me up and let me stand.*
> *On the mountain tops of Glory,*
> *let me dwell in Beulah land.*
> *Lift me up above the shadows*
> *when the storms are raging high . . .*
> *Lift me up above my grief, Lord,*

give me g ld for my alloy...
Lift me up 'till the storms of life are past...
'Till we stand in Heaven at last!"

In the difficult years that followed, my parents would comfort themselves many more times by singing that song. But they had both now laid the cornerstone for a life together that would be filled with a new power.

2

NATURAL LIVING

IN RECONSTRUCTING THE events of my extraordinary birth, I've developed a growing understanding of the way God works in our lives. I see now that this miracle irrevocably put His mark on my life—and the lives of my parents. He claimed us. As His restored children, there was much He wanted to teach us. But how patient He is!

The first lessons came during the harsh Depression of the 1930s. It took my parents seven years to pay for Mother's and my hospital expenses. They prayed for work to provide money to put food on the table. Then the phone would ring and the caller would offer Dad an electrical job.

When bills arrived, they prayed for funds. On occasion, my grandparents would pay our bills. Or more odd jobs would come to my father. At one time or another every member of our family felt an inner "stirring" to help someone else who was in need. The "Stirrer," of course, was God.

At one low point soon after my brother Don was born, our last potato was gone and there was no work lined up. Dad walked out the back door with the last shotgun shell in his left hand and his gun over his right shoulder. For one panicky moment Mother feared he would use it on himself, he was so defeated at not being able to provide properly for his family. Things were so bad for every family that all the small game in the nearby wooded areas seemed to have been captured or shot.

Mother moaned when she heard the blast of the shotgun. Daddy soon came running up the walk holding one very skinny rabbit, probably the only one left in all of Vigo County. It made a dinner for three.

An elderly man once gave Mother a bag of half-rotted oranges. We salvaged the good portions and had another meal.

A neighbor hoarded a large quantity of rice too long and weevils got into it. She gave Mother a box of it to feed to the birds. Mother boiled the rice slowly. The weevils floated to the top. She skimmed off the weevils, put them out for the birds, and we ate the rice. Another meal.

Then there was the night my father gave his testimony in a nearby church about Mother's healing. They took up a love offering for us. There was twenty-three cents in the offering plate. On the way home we learned that Mother had given a nickel of that.

That night we knelt beside the bed, Mother on one side, Daddy on the other with me in the middle. My baby brother Don was asleep in his borrowed crib. Daddy thanked God for the twenty-three cents. That would provide milk and bread for breakfast. Bread was five cents a loaf, and milk was twelve cents a quart. Mother needed nourishment badly for she was nursing Don.

While we were kneeling, we heard a scratching sound at the front door. Mother and Dad stared at each other, wide-eyed with fear. Sensing their tension, I started to cry out. Mother put her hand over my mouth, while Daddy slipped a strong arm around me, and Mother whispered in my ear,

"People are breaking into houses to steal food. When they see that we don't have anything either, they will leave, don't worry." We didn't even have a cake of ice in the icebox. The old refrigerator had been turned off months before, since we could no longer pay the utility bill.

When the noise stopped, Daddy cautiously opened the door to the porch. There he stumbled onto a large, cardboard box. I'll always remember what was in it—a ham, two quarts of milk, a bottle of orange juice, a loaf of bread, a pound of butter. What a good bedtime meal we had—several slices of bread with butter, and glasses of cold, fresh milk. Milk had never tasted so good!

One of the songs of the era that sums up those years was sung by Ray Stevens: "Everybody needs a Mama and a Papa that will take enough time to play, take enough time to pray." I'm glad mine taught me how to pray through the desperate 1930s.

They were indeed difficult, yes, even desperate years. Dependent times. But a period when God was very close to us—as He always is when and where there is need.

I still remember the feeling of excitement in my parents as the Lord met each small crisis. There was no over-emotion about it, few dramatics. He was there with us in a very natural way. Somehow the closer we were to nature, the closer we were to Him.

Then came a significant event. My father moved quite naturally from a life of working with his hands into a life of meeting the needs of people as a pastor.

The way it happened is what makes it significant. My father didn't stop doing physical work. As he ministered to other people, he would do small carpentry or repair jobs for them. When he refitted a door, built a shelf or repaired the leg of a table for his parishioners, he also counseled them about their problems much as Jesus might have done in His role of a carpenter nearly two thousand years ago.

As a pastor my father continued to do what was natural for

him—work with his hands. To the *natural* he added something *super*—bringing God's love and joy and power into the lives of needy people.

What a great blending of forces! Super natural living. One is dependent on the other.

But this exciting discovery has only come to me in recent years. When younger, I wanted to do all my living in the natural world as most other young people were doing. There's nothing terribly wrong with this, of course. When God created the world, He called it "Good." He made it for us, His children. But living only in the natural world is living a fifty-percent life. It's like living half-dead, which is worse to me than being dead. The other fifty percent comes when we bring the full power of God into our daily life.

How do you do that?

It varies from situation to situation, as I have discovered.

Today we're all concerned about the economy. How are we going to pay our bills? How can we stretch our money to cover our needs?

The natural way is to reduce spending, stick to a budget. Save and economize. Be more disciplined. Get out of debt. All are right and in order. But some days we do, and some days we fall short.

There is a better way. Go the natural route, but add something to it. God's dimension. Bring Him into our economic problems and ask His help. God pays all bills which He has authorized.

After Carl Malz and I were married, he changed his career several times in the next eight years. The fact that Carl was always a conscientious provider didn't keep us from going through some severe economic ups and downs. After doing all the natural things to cut our costs, we prayed for help. God was faithful.

Once our bank account was at zero and it was six days before Carl would be paid. I prayed, "Lord, I need a fifty-pound bag of horse feed, and 100 postage stamps to send out my mail. We need milk, coffee, bread, cheese, and some potatoes." The following day I received in the mail a check for $31.00. It was a payment due me for books I had provided months before and then had forgotten. It arrived the day I really needed it. When payday came, I still had sixteen cents left over.

A short time later, a large printing bill was due on Tuesday. I spoke at a church on Sunday night. The offering was four cents over the amount of the printing bill.

On another occasion we were down to zero funds and again it was two weeks before payday. All we had to eat were vegetables and fruit which we had grown and frozen. I prayed, "Lord, please supply some meat." The following Monday at noon, Carl spoke at the Kiwanis Club luncheon. Art Sather, the program chairman, came up to him afterward and said, "We don't give an honorarium, Carl, but I have something for you." He gave Carl a box of his special, corn-fed, prize-project beef!

This past summer I ran short on cash. Then I noticed two trees that hadn't borne fruit the first summer we arrived, but were now bearing apricots. We had apricots on cereal at breakfast, apricot preserves for lunch and apricot upside-down cake for dessert at dinner. Then an idea came and I took a basket of apricots to a local grocery where I received $22.00 for them.

I was pitching hay over the fence to our two horses recently when I noticed that our hay supply was almost gone. With our long, cold winters the rainfall is not always adequate to grow enough hay. I prayed, "Lord, please provide us some good quality hay that we can afford. You know it's still two weeks until payday."

Two hours later, I noticed a flat bed truck parked in the middle of the road in front of the house. Several rolls of hay had fallen off, blocking a lane of traffic. The driver came to the door.

"Lady, if you can get on the phone and locate someone with

a front loader, I'll appreciate this. We have to deliver this hay before dark."

It took six calls. Finally, I located a farmer who agreed to help. While cooking dinner, I glanced out and saw them securing the hay on the truck with cables. But there was still one roll left on the road. As I watched, the men took this large, 1,100-pound roll of green, rich hay and lowered it gently in front of our feed lot.

Next morning in the early light I didn't have to get close to smell the clover and alfalfa in it. The horses were already leaning over the fence, eager for a mouthful. That hay was a true, "my God shall supply all your needs" answer.

I realize that our situation can't be compared with what people face in real poverty and with real hunger, but the principle is the same. When we are in a state of lack — big or small — God loves us so much that He wants to provide for us. The key point is that we need to seek Him, to ask Him, to love Him, and to show our gratitude; otherwise we become lopsided wheels on a bumpy ride through life.

The practice of this principle gets us in the flow of His power. Again, super natural living. The natural is the door to the spiritual. Both are of the same cloth, created by the same God who, when incarnated, was both natural and spiritual.

I received a letter recently from my dad, Glenn Perkins. "I'm going to be seventy-five in January," he wrote. "The Bible says that 'the Just shall live by faith,' that they shall *survive* by their faith. Though I live on Social Security, I am completely dependent on Spiritual Security — God's Welfare. That's the way we lived back in the Depression of the 1930s and that's the kind of living I can really depend on."

Our survival depends on how real God is to us. Yet so few people believe that today. With our government over one trillion dollars in debt, what happens when there's an attempt to cut down expenses? A scream of anguish that makes all our elected representatives tremble. We are a nation of people addicted to a high standard of living; anyone who dares trim this down is threatened with everything short of bodily injury and death.

The sad truth is that God is shut out of all this, just as He was by His chosen people years ago. When the Israelites escaped their Egyptian captors for a new life in a new land, God promised to take care of them. And He did—in a supernatural way. Their feet did not swell, nor did their shoes wear out! When they hungered, He provided a savory dew called Manna, then flocks of quail. This was His promise:

> "For the Lord your God is bringing you into a good land, a land of brooks of water, of fountains and springs, flowing forth in valleys and hills, a land of wheat and barley, of vines and fig trees and pomegranates, a land of olive trees and honey, a land in which you will eat bread without scarcity, in which you will lack nothing, a land whose stones are iron, and out of whose hills you can dig copper. And you shall eat and be full, and you shall bless the Lord your God for the good land He has given you" (Deuteronomy 8:7-10, RSV).

God also made it possible for the Israelites to defeat their enemies in battle. Yet God's chosen people ended up constantly grumbling, wishing that they were back in the "flesh pots" of Egypt, even rejecting Him to worship pleasure and worthless idols. This so displeased God that He withdrew His supernatural protection and soon the Israelites were back in captivity, this time under the Babylonians.

There is no question that this nation has been blessed by God in as many ways as were the Israelites back in the time of King David. If we as a nation turn to Him today, and in a spirit of repentance and self-sacrifice will invest in prayer, asking for His help and protection, God will bless us again with His abundance.

As my family is learning to trust God for our needs, we are also trying to save in natural, little ways. Here are some things I do:

1. When a tube of toothpaste seems squeezed out, I take a razor blade, split the tube with it and get another four more brushings. When my lotion bottle seems empty, I turn it upside down, resting it on the lid. There is always more inside than I had thought.

2. I take tiny, leftover soap slivers, set them on a window sill in a saucer in the sun until they are warm. Then I press them together into one, usable bar of soap.

3. We save electricity by using candles more often, hanging the laundry on clothes lines, going to bed earlier and arising earlier. Since a kitchen stove can burn a lot of electricity, we had an iron arm installed in the wall of the fireplace. Now I can make soup, chili, roasts and stew on the open fire. Needing a second bathroom, we came up with an ingenious solution — we found an old outdoor toilet in good condition. A neighbor helped us install it between the feed shed and the dog kennel. While this is no answer for city people, it is for those of us living in the country. It's quiet out there with no phone.

4. We save on fuel bills by turning the thermostat down. I have sweaters hanging on all the doorknobs, wear wool socks, heavy house-slippers and wool slacks around the house. By eating more raw fruits and vegetables, we save energy and gain the added fibre for better health.

5. I shop at a grocery discount center. It means buying in larger quantities, but the savings are considerable.

6. We are exploring the barter system so that if a national emergency comes, we will know how to trade what we grow, or no longer use, for tools and services.

7. We had a garage sale recently and made $312.00 selling items from the attic, garage and my clothes closet, which we weren't using but other people needed.

8. I'm supplementing our family income by writing. Others can do such income-producing things in the home as typing, telephone-selling, sewing, trading baby-sitting instead of hiring or paying for this service.

Undergird these natural suggestions with the spiritual by memorizing Scripture promises such as the following:

"Let them shout for joy and be glad . . . Let the Lord be magnified, which hath pleasure in the prosperity of his servant" (Psalm 35:27).

"In the days of famine, they shall be satisfied" (Psalm 37:19).

"Wait on the Lord, and keep his way, and he shall exalt thee to inherit the land" (Psalm 37:34).

"Let thy loving kindness and thy truth continually preserve me" (Psalm 40:11).

"Lo, I [Jesus] am with you always, even unto the end of the world" (Matthew 28:20).

3

FAMILY ALTAR

WHEN GOD FIRST created Adam, He knew it was unnatural for man to be alone. So He created Eve as his companion. And it was quite natural for them to become one flesh and produce children.

Whence came the family.

But what God made to be natural and good between husband and wife, He decreed as unnatural outside of marriage. That so many have disagreed and disobeyed this divine pronouncement over the centuries hasn't changed God's mind one bit. He knows what works and what doesn't work in marriage and in the home.

What is natural between man and woman is good, but it doesn't become truly satisfying and fulfilling unless the spiritual — the "super" — is added. Yet, throughout the world, the percentage of homes with that super natural quality is very small. The result:

Worldwide, family living is in shambles.
The home is a combat zone.
Most marriages now break up.

These are the devastating statements you hear over and over today. Few will care to dispute them, for the divorce statistics are frightening.

How grieved God must be to see so much wreckage of lives when His solution is both obvious and available. Yet I know personally how easy it is to get off the course He has provided.

I began my marriage to John Upchurch expecting to be loved, cherished and cared for, in return for which I would maintain the home and bear children. John was a devoted husband. But I was more concerned at times with what I would get out of marriage rather than what I could give, and I was often dissatisfied. Always, I seemed to be reaching for more. We were believers and church-goers, but God did not come first in our lives.

John's death from a heart attack was a deep shock. Belatedly, I realized what a generous, loving, giving man he had been and how my self-centeredness kept us from having the maximum kind of marriage God wanted and intended us to have.

Carl Malz also lost his mate through death. We met and married in an exciting romance, which brought two broken homes together, including my two children, April and Brenda, and his daughter, Connie. April described it as the time "we all got married" since she, at age five, was the ring bearer, while Brenda, fifteen, stood beside me and Connie, fourteen, beside Carl—all of us in front of the altar.

I think Carl and I assumed that, since we were both Christians and experienced at this marriage business, we would automatically be successful.

Wrong.

In *Prayers That Are Answered,* I described how different we were in temperament, habits and general lifestyle. We needed an extra, spiritual dimension to make the necessary adjustments, and got it. But not without some painful experiences.

Looking back now after eight years of marriage, I feel much love and understanding toward Carl, combined with a sorrowful regret when I was not more sensitive to his situation. After our marriage he was called upon to make more new adjustments than were humanly possible. First he accepted a new job, then moved to a new state, meanwhile absorbing three new people into his family, all with opposite natures and dispositions from his own.

Carl is a technical perfectionist, a city person, accustomed to a cosmopolitan outlook and challenges, and felt it necessary to plan his daughter's day for her. My two girls and I have been country people surrounded by the outdoors, animals and pets. My children had lived in an unstructured environment and were allowed to roam about leisurely.

Carl's first wife, Wanda, was an immaculate housekeeper and lived to help other people. I like music, writing, reading, gardening, animals — especially horses and collies — and outdoor sports. Obviously too many interests. I love to cook and bake, but not clean house.

I have always been frugal. Carl is generous—with himself and others.

Despite the fact that we had positions of Christian leadership—Carl as a counselor, teacher, pastor and I as a speaker, columnist and author—we began to clash more and more. Some of our scenes were silly, some hilarious. All were emotional. The one we laugh about most today is the one we call "The Ump," which climaxed a week of upsets.

It started one Saturday morning with my vacuuming the downstairs while Carl was in his study nearby preparing his Sunday morning sermon. When he protested about the noise, I stopped the vacuum and began to wallpaper the dining room. This, too, was going against Carl's wishes; he wanted to hire professionals to do it. I was sure this would be a waste of money.

Soon I was not only blocking traffic, but my inexperience caused me to drop pails and rollers. Carl finally stormed out again. "Must we tear the house apart this particular morning?" he began.

"This is the one free morning I have for house projects," I replied.

"Why can't it wait?"

"Because I have all the materials here now. And the dining room looks like a barn without wall paper."

"I like barns. I like the dining room just fine the way it is." Carl's voice was tense.

"I think it looks dull, flat, boring."

Somehow this exchange brought to a head all the difficulties we had been going through for a period of months. His fuse blew. "That's it!" he shouted. "From now on you will be alone to run things the way you want to. We're...."

Then very dramatically he bent forward like an umpire about to give the "out" signal, his forehead almost touching the carpet, his legs spread apart, his long arms spread across his 205-pound body. Abruptly he jerked his head up, his arms flung wide as he shouted: "...through!" (emphasizing thrrrrr-ough). Then he strode back to his study.

It was an impressive performance. As I watched him retire again to his work, I was devastated: was the marriage really over? I left the dining room only half-finished and went to the bedroom to sulk. Carl finished his work and drove into town returning at the end of the afternoon. Dinner that evening was very quiet. Neither of us had anything to say. Long after the others were asleep, I lay awake—thinking.

I prayed silently, *Lord, I am not adequate or qualified to be a mother and wife in this situation. I feel like giving up. I've never lived when I had to worry about hurting someone's feelings all the time. I hate being so cautious. I've already changed so much, I feel like a chameleon. I hardly know me anymore. Lord, please, I need help.*

Then I heard a crackling sound downstairs. I looked over at Carl. He had not awakened. Quietly, I put on my robe and slippers and tiptoed down the steps. Perhaps the fire in the dining room fireplace was out of control.

Then I froze. I didn't even have to turn on the light. From the doorway, I could see the problem by the moonlight streaming through the windows. The newly hung wallpaper in the dining room was slowly peeling off and sliding down the wall. One strip had completely separated from the wall and was on the floor.

I had worked so hard on this project I was heartsick. But I didn't cry. Numbness set in for a moment. Then I padded into the dining room, found an empty package of the paste mixture and, using my flashlight, read the instructions again. I had used an improper sizing on the wall. That's why it did not stick.

As I stood there, another strip of wallpaper fell on the floor. Then another began to peel off. I reached for it—too late.

Then the lesson hit me. We five people in this household were not holding together either. *Thank you, God, for this truth,* I prayed, then asked for the right glue to put our family back together. Turning from my "handyman's disaster," I went upstairs and fell exhausted into bed.

The next day, I saddled our bay mare and rode slowly around the perimeter of our thirty-eight acre pasture, letting the breeze in the cool morning air blow the cobwebs from my stale, traditional tunnel-visioned thinking. Why was I so over zealous to do everything *now?* I was robbing my husband of his peace and our children of the quiet flow of a smooth-running home. There was a proper rhythm of life and we were not synchronized to it.

As I listened to God that morning, I heard Him say that He was the key to harmonious living in the home. If all members of the family were submitted to Him, there would be harmony and love and fun together. If we took our eyes off

Him, the enemy would move in with his bag full of strife, resentment, jealousy, self-pity—all the little tricks that upset a home.

As I walked inside our house, Carl came out of his study, reached out his big arms and held me tight. "We're gonna make it!" he whispered.

We sat down, feeling weak, as if we had been through an exhausting match with a strong, unseen foe. We had come through a spiritual war. I asked his forgiveness for my high-handed ways.

Carl confessed that he had become too image-conscious at the college where he taught, that because he was receiving such respect and enthusiasm from his students, he had been giving *them* his best. He was serving us, his family, the leftovers. He realized now that this was why we were not respecting him as he felt we should. We were giving him our leftover attention because he was serving us his leftover patience, wit and charm, his leftover time and energy.

It was a wonderful moment of reconciliation. Out of it came the decision to put God first in our home. One way to do this, we decided, was to center more on *the family altar.*

My parents and grandparents had maintained closely knit families and as I relived my youth, a host of memories flooded over me. One of the earliest was when I first felt the presence of the Holy Spirit. It did not happen in church, but it came while I was praying with my maternal grandparents, Mom and Dad Burns, in their home.

I stayed overnight with them many times. Each night before bedtime, we all gathered in the living room. If they had guests, they were invited to join the family. My grandfather would read a short portion from the Bible, then we would kneel for prayer. I always sat beside my youngest aunt, Pearl Irene, on the bottom step of the stairway leading upstairs. This step was our favorite pew—just the right height to substitute for our altar or kneeling bench.

Around the room, starting with the oldest and on down to

the very youngest, each one of us prayed aloud about anything on our hearts. Once, I felt such a powerful warmth in my heart that tears came to my eyes. I didn't understand about the Holy Spirit then, but I certainly learned to pray in public without fear and with confidence that God was listening.

Likewise, we did this in my parents' home, too, while I was growing up. Without fail, each night before retiring, we had what we called "family altar." As I look back I recall some miraculous answers to those prayers, a few in connection with our school studies. These prayers helped to fortify my brothers and me against criticism, ridicule and disappointment in the world.

The Word and prayer we received during those family altar times was like a vaccination. We were not isolated from the world, but insulated by prayer. When we were exposed to sin, temptation and immorality, it wouldn't "take" on us. All five of us—my four brothers and I—have wavered, but we have all returned to the Source of power and strength to establish and sustain our own homes.

So Carl and I established a family altar in our newly-formed home for the five members of our family. Each day, a different family member would read one short page from a devotional book. Then we knelt together to pray. It is difficult to ridicule someone you are praying for and kneeling beside. Carl would slip an arm around me, or I would reach for his hand. After each member prayed aloud, one at a time, we would close in a concerted prayer of praise to Jesus. Those times were always like a breath of fresh air to us.

As a result of these family altar times, all of us began to apologize for certain wrong feelings or hidden grievances. This not only brought me closer to my step-daughter, but enabled me to help her through a major crisis in her life.

Connie was developing into a beautiful young woman. The summer she was seventeen, she eagerly accepted a job as life guard at a youth camp. In this way, she met a young, tanned boy who loved to sail his boat close to the shore where the campers were swimming.

When she returned home, she informed us that she did not want to finish high school. She had fallen in love with this boy, whom we'll call Larry, and she was going to marry him. At first we were shocked, then hurt. Her father told her it was a summer romance and it would pass. But it did not. Larry called her often, and then wrote to tell her that his parents thought their getting married was fine and would help them select an apartment and some furniture.

Realizing she would not be talked out of it, we prayed for Larry and then invited him to spend Thanksgiving weekend in our home. After two days, Connie's interest in Larry had obviously cooled. He no longer had his suntan and was not a conversationalist. He looked at our family with a strange expression when we talked of God. He obviously felt awkward during our family altar time. He seemed to have no plans to get a job. Though he was sweet and lovable, after he left we felt sure that Connie would see what a mistake it would be to marry him. But there was pride involved and she seemed determined to proceed with the marriage.

I decided that my role was simply to pray. Many nights I stood at her bedroom door after she'd closed it and prayed, "Lord, help her."

One morning as she left for school, she kissed me goodbye and gave me a letter to mail to Larry. I held it in my hands, raised it heavenward and prayed for the young man and for Connie. God would make happen what was best and right for these two young people.

A passage of Scripture I read that morning was reassuring: "You shall know that the living God is among you" (Joshua 3:10).

That same morning, I had a sudden and strange feeling. I had never met Connie's mother, who had died before Carl and I were married, but I suddenly became aware that *her* prayers were strengthening me. Carl had told me that before Wanda died, she had talked about his remarriage. "Please pick a good mother to take my place, a *caring* one, a praying one who will help fashion Connie into an honorable woman, wife and mother," she had pleaded.

With all the faith I could muster, I prayed, "Lord, please answer Wanda's prayer. I love her daughter. Now she is *my* daughter. I won't nag, but trust You to intervene in a supernatural way. You are the God of nature, and the God who controls even natural desires such as love."

A warm reassurance flooded me that this child, born to missionaries, schooled well in the Bon Pasteur French School in Cairo, would not waste her life, would not make this dreadful mistake, but would see the Light and follow it as she had been taught to do.

One morning many days later, when Connie did not come downstairs for breakfast after her alarm went off, I went to check on her. Only a mother can know the suspicious thought I entertained when she told me she was nauseated and too sick to get up. As I started to leave her room, I looked more closely and saw that she had broken out with chicken pox. Feeling her head, I discovered that she had a high fever. A call to her school confirmed the fact that she had been exposed to chicken pox.

During the fourth day of her confinement, Connie called me to her room. I sat on the rug by her bed while she drank some lemonade I had taken to her. I could tell that she had been crying. From under the pillow she pulled out an envelope. "Mother, would you please cash in this ticket, and get my money refunded? I had planned to elope for a Christmas wedding. Can you help me get out of this? I don't want to hurt Larry, but I can't go through with this. We have so few things in common. I know now that it isn't right."

I hugged her. She made a brief phone call to Larry explaining that she had chicken pox and couldn't come there for Christmas. I then sat down and helped her write Larry a letter with a full explanation of why she was calling off their marriage plans.

The payoff for me came on my next birthday when I found this note scotch-taped to my pillow:

Mom,

Not so many years ago, you came into my world. I was hurting, and you soothed the hurt. You went further than that—you brought laughter, encouragement and faith. You gave me another family to belong to when I had lost my own. You taught me to love again during a time in my life when love was just a word. My walls were crashing in, but you helped to build them up.

Let me give back to you a little of the precious things you gave me. Let me help you laugh and let me pick up some of your burdens to call my own. If ever your world starts to crumble, call on me. I will help you with love, giving you back the love you gave me when you came into my world. Happy Birthday, Mother!

Love,
Connie.

Connie is now married to a handsome young man who had already graduated from college and had a good job when they met. Steven Bobzien is a loving, Christian husband, in charge of the youth athletic program in their church, and is the father of their Jared, now four, and baby twins, Joshua and Indie (a boy and a girl). We are all thrilled!

Brenda, too, met and married a wonderful young man named Bud Smart. They have two adorable children, Erika and Ryan.

And how great it is that Connie and Brenda, both so close in age, have become not just step-sisters but friends. They exchange motherly advice, letters full of warmth, and borrow maternity clothes from each other.

God has honored the prayers that flowed to Him during our family altar time. As the spiritual emphasis of our family came into balance, He directed us again toward those natural things that enrich life.

The produce from our garden began providing a surprising percentage of our food needs. April, for example, planted a pumpkin patch and made a $26.00 profit on it. We acquired an old coffee mill. Carl and I are up before daylight to enjoy the smell of freshly ground beans and the aroma of their brewing as we eat breakfast by candlelight.

By choice, we have an old-fashioned crank-style ice cream freezer because there is more fellowship when we crank than when we push a button. More and more, we are replacing our electric gadgets with manual devices.

The aroma of whole wheat bread baking in the oven fills the house regularly. The recipe came, surprisingly, not from "granny" but my daughter Brenda. It costs little for me to bake two or four loaves at a time. The Prophet Jeremiah was on target when he told us, ". . . ask for the old paths, where is the good way, and walk therein, and ye shall find rest for your souls" (Jeremiah 6:16).

The evening meal in our house becomes the focal point of the day because this is the one time we are all together for an hour or more. Preparation for this can begin in the morning with the gathering of vegetables from the garden, chopping of wood, the purchase of supplies.

By late afternoon, it's time to light the fire in the dining room fireplace. It's hard for family members to shout at each other, or get angry while lying on their stomachs in front of a flickering fire of apple wood logs with a few pine cones tossed in for scent.

Sometimes I light the old red and crystal kerosene lamps in the kitchen while working because it adds such a nostalgic, old-fashioned touch and is such a good change from the sameness of the electric light. Furthermore, it reminds me of one of my favorite Scriptures, Proverbs 20:27, "The spirit of man is the candle of the Lord."

I've discovered the use of candles to be important. When

two candles are flickering silently in the middle of the dining table, it's very hard to be quarrelsome and loud. What is there about candles that brings such warmth, atmosphere and spirituality to any occasion?

Music, too, is important in creating the right atmosphere. Records for our stereo are selected with one purpose in mind — to bring to the meal peace, harmony and holiness. One record we play often is Big John Hall singing in his bass voice, "Peace in the Midst of the Storm," providing a soft background for our dinnertime conversation. And what happens at the dinner table leads into the family altar time afterwards, when we seek the wisdom of Scripture and pray together.

On special occasions, we end the evening meal with a communion service. Carl leads us in the breaking of the Bread and the drinking from the Cup while flickering candlelight casts its golden glow over us all.

I realize that in many families today both parents hold down jobs. Working wives therefore cannot spend each day preparing the home for a family time in the evening. If it is essential that the wife works—and I think the reason should be stronger than her need for self-expression, or just extra money—then she is going to have to use extra creativity and the close help and support of her husband and children to produce an atmosphere of family togetherness.

It can be done, of course, if both parents are determined to put God first and use prayer as the force that heals, reconciles and binds members together.

Super natural living for the family is that perfect blend of what God has given us: the beauty and bounty of His great outdoors, plus the gifts of laughter, love, song, and worship that pour from our hearts.

4

WINGS AND FEET

My life is testimony to the fact that I believe in the super natural power of God to change people and to alter our circumstances today.

I was stillborn and prayed into life. Twenty-seven years later, I was pronounced dead in my hospital bed, given a marvelous preview of eternal life, then returned to this world to serve Him further. I am everlastingly grateful that the Lord has filled me with His Spirit and equipped me with gifts to minister to other people.

Yet I still glory in the natural world all about us. I scrub my kitchen floor, clean our toilets, shovel out the manure in our stable. As I bake, cook, clean, weed and dig in the earth, I feel joy and satisfaction in these everyday tasks.

Keeping my balance between the spiritual and natural worlds seems very important. But as I've traveled about the country during the past ten years and viewed the movement of the Holy Spirit in people and churches, I've been dismayed at how out-of-balance some people appear. In fact, I've encountered a regular procession of Sainted Sallies, square halos, Dolly-Do-Goods, lopsided wheels, false faces, sacred clowns and Christian "palm readers."

For example, I was backstage behind the curtain at a civic center auditorium recently, with about two minutes left before I was to speak. Seconds before the curtain opened, a woman who looked like a drill sergeant for the Women's Army Corps marched up to me and pinned a white orchid on my left shoulder. Then, while I was being announced and just before the curtain went up, she pulled out an overly long, silver-safety pin and closed the front of my beige lace dress.

Then with a knowing, "starched" smile she affirmed, "It's nice to have them, but we wouldn't want to show them now, would we?"

I am so tall (almost "five feet, twelve inches"), most people have to look up to see me, and from the high platform where I was standing, a man would have to hang from the rafters to see down the neck of my dress. It really wasn't cut that low besides. Her reprimand almost paralyzed me. For several, long moments, I stood before the audience nonplused, struggling with my opening remarks. The looks of acceptance and anticipation on the faces of the people in the filled auditorium slowly erased the memory of my encounter with that self-appointed, diagnostic Sainted Sally, and I was able to regain my composure.

I've met people who are super but not natural; weird but far from wonderful; fancy but not functional; pretty but not practical; spooky but not spiritual. God's ways are often hard to understand, but they are not far out. It is Satan's role to try and distort and corrupt all good things. If he can't side-track us from lifting up Jesus, he will steer us into super-spiritual works. For example, he loves to busy us with Satan-stomping, devil-denouncing meetings so that we become promoters of a Super-Satan, with no time to discern our brother's natural need.

I speak here out of personal experience. The reason I so

quickly recognize these imbalanced people is that I have been there—and could lose my balance again at any time unless I'm careful. At the age of twenty-three, for example, I was a typical Dolly-Do-Good.

I scorched many a pot of coffee and burned many dishes in the oven while listening to people pour out their troubles to me so that I could appear adequate to solve them.

I remember one particular evening when I tried to do my good deed of helping a person when I should have recommended a minister or psychiatrist. I was getting ready to french fry shrimp when the phone rang. While giving advice, I let the grease on the stove overheat to combustion temperature. By the time I finished talking, the kitchen was in flames, and I had to escape by the side door.

On the way home from work, seeing the smoke and hearing the siren of the fire truck, my husband was heard to remark, "It's probably my house. My wife is talented at playing God on the phone to callers, and forgets her natural duties."

He was right. The repair job cost $2,400 to restore the cabinets and the stove and window above it.

I should have been arrested for malpractice. My husband calmly but surely gave me an ultimatum, "Play in your own field. Stick to your own vocation and talk about things you know. If you don't, I'm going to buy you a cot and move you into the church office where you can 'do good' twenty-four hours a day."

I'm glad I heeded. I enjoyed working with my hands, and enjoyed being a mother. I took time to do John's bookkeeping for the business, to go boating and water skiing with him, and waited beside the fireplace long hours for his return home from work when he would have to stay late, just to be with him. Until his death following heart surgery, he was a very natural, loving person, and he helped me find a good balance between the super and natural.

Over the years, I've learned that if I stay in my own natural environment, looking to God for direction, He is sure to get me involved in His super natural department. For I'm convinced that He is looking for "naturals" through which to manifest His miraculous power. He used ordinary people through which to channel His extraordinary.

Some people try so hard to be "super Christians." However, some try so hard that they mess up their marriages. My present husband, Carl, spent hours counselling one wife who was very frustrated. Night after night she would bathe, dab herself with perfume and don her blue lace gown while her husband would sit with the bed lamp on until midnight writing religious poetry.

I'm sure he got brownie points for his spirituality, but to me he was being unnatural, unhealthy and probably in need of vitamins.

I chuckled when I read the over-exaggerated account of the young groom whose wife was getting ready to retire for the night. She put her eyelashes and her wig in the second drawer. Beside them she laid her padded foam bra, her tinted contact lenses, her artificial fingernails, her makeup and platform shoes—all in the second drawer.

His question was, "When I want to be near Meg, shall I crawl into bed, or into that second drawer?"

Super natural living, as it is empowered by the Holy Spirit, scarcely requires artificial flavor, coloring or synthetics.

Ruby was a real lopsided wheel. Her theme song was not "Rescue The Perishing," but "I don't smoke, I don't chew, and I don't speak to folks who do." Her credo was, "cleanliness *is* godliness." As a result, her husband became a discouraged man. Their living room was not for living but for looking. The red velvet chairs were covered with white sheets to keep them like new. Her kitchen was fancy but not functional—a display center for her copperware, Corningware and Noritake china.

The bedroom was not for loving but for looking, too. Ruby

wouldn't let her husband kiss her when he rushed in from work until he first combed his hair, brushed his teeth and shaved. To me, she is an unnatural mannequin in a showroom window — for display only.

Rick called my husband to ask for prayer for his shapely, little Italian wife. He wanted her to go to church with him and know God in the powerful way he did.

One session with this wife revealed that she was repulsed by his super-spirituality. He prayed so loud for her during the night that his bellowing sometimes awakened their two small children. He asserted his spiritual authority so often that she decided he was more interested in being boss than being right. My husband's conclusion: when a man spends all his time calling fouls, it leaves little time to play the game—or to score with his mate.

This one ended well. Rick accepted stern counsel, learned that a good husband mixes temperance with godliness and sweet courtesies. He and his wife now happily go to church together and act as a team in rearing their children in a Christ-centered home.

Henry was desperate when he came to the pastor of our church to ask for a most unusual prayer.

"I'm married to a supernatural bore," he began. "I want you to pray that God will take this 'angel' home to Glory and replace her with a flesh-and-blood wife who will cook and be a natural mother for our children."

The pastor was startled by the request and told Henry he couldn't pray that type of prayer for anyone. Henry then went on to describe Lila, his wife, this way: "She is constantly taking the spiritual temperature of others. She usually acts terribly depressed, saying that she has a burden for prayer. She always has a headache, so I think her halo is too tight. She can't eat, won't cook, can't sleep, especially with me. She has lost weight and looks like the 'wrath of God.' Maybe that's why she shuts herself in her room away from the kids and me to talk to God. She can't function naturally because she is so 'super.' When I try to be affectionate, she replies, 'Some people like watermelon, and some don't. I don't.'"

The pastor's talk with Lila produced a surprising result. Lila agreed to visit her medical doctor. The exam revealed that she was anemic. After iron shots and food supplements, she perked up and became a real wife in both super and natural ways.

There's a parallel to this in the Bible story of Elijah who became depressed, saying, "Lord, take my life, I just want to die." In his case, depression was merely deflated ego. After the angel came and fed Elijah, he caught up on his sleep, regained his ebbing strength, stabilized his mental condition, got a new vision of power and lived many more years.

I am troubled by the people who try to be prophets when that is not their gift. For eighteen months, my mother lay dying before she lost her battle with cancer. We had wonderful support from positive, praying visitors. These prayers sustained Mother and encouraged our whole family. Unfortunately, two well-meaning people laid hands on Mother and prayed for her, which was fine, but then they spoke a "prophecy" that she would get well soon and once again be the right hand of help my dad needed.

This turned out to be a false prophecy. Though our hopes had been raised for several weeks, Mother died shortly thereafter. Many times people are guilty of saying in the form of prophecy what they think people want to hear. This is presumption. God will not be manipulated. Sometimes He heals miraculously, sometimes not. God's ways, I've discovered, are unfathomable but always for our greater good.

Then there are those who confuse faith with superstition and look for signs and wonders as their faith builders. An executive in his late forties felt lonely after his wife's death and began praying that God would send him a suitable mate. Driving to his office one day, he noticed that the mileage indicator on his new car had rolled up the number 777 just as he parked. He had always felt that "seven" was his lucky number.

"That's it," he thought. "God's telling me I'll find her today." Going up the stairs of the professional building two steps at a time, the first person he said "good morning" to was a young secretary about twenty years his junior, whom he had always admired.

Surprised and delighted, he impulsively shared his mystical revelation with this young woman. She was not only "turned off," but whispered it to others on the staff, nearly jeopardizing the man's credibility and his job.

The problem with people like this is that in their superspirituality they are divorcing the spiritual from what is real.

Jesus is our perfect example of super natural living. While on earth He was closely tied to the things of this world—both the drab and the beautiful—and referred to them often in His teachings: lilies in the fields, the vine, a lost sheep, the thief in the night, good seed, bad soil. I don't think these things of daily life were just analogies for Jesus. I believe He saw the Father in wildflowers and birds and shepherds caring for sheep.

Jesus was simply profound because he was so profoundly simple. Most of His three years of ministry were spent walking. He walked the seashore; He climbed the hills. As a carpenter, He learned early in life to make things with His hands. He was adept with tools. He liked to fish, and was not too lofty spiritually to clean the catch and cook breakfast for His disciples.

Jesus willingly spoke to multitudes, or to one woman by a well. He loved to be with children. He gravitated toward need. He invested in people instead of things. The common people of the earth were His sisters and brothers. He was angered by the super-pious Pharisees and Sadducees, who prayed so loudly and self-righteously in public and were so filled with their spirituality that they were horrified when He dared to heal the sick on the sabbath.

In His speech, Jesus tried to lead people away from hard and fast dogmas; doctrine never crept into His language. He explored the mystery of life in images the world will never forget through a device we call the parable. What He said seemed so natural and earthy and obvious, with an incomparable economy of words, yet the total impact was supernatural with depths no one else has ever matched.

While my husband Carl was teaching at Trinity Bible Institute in Ellendale, North Dakota, he discovered how quickly young people can become super-spiritual from too much concentrated, heavy thinking. It usually happened in February, when bad weather kept the students indoors for weeks at a time. The overly pious became judgmental, self-righteous, insensitive to others. The less pious became depressed. Everyone gained weight.

Carl solved the problem by forming the "One Hundred Mile Club." All were encouraged to meet at 6:00 each morning. First, they prayed until 6:30. From 6:30 until 7:00, they ran, jogged, or walked briskly. A chart/graph was posted, and when a member completed the 100 miles, he or she received a trophy.

The praying lifted their spirits; the fresh cool air swept the mist from their thinking minds; and their bodies lost fat. Soon it became known as "Wings and Feet" (pray and run).

Super natural living includes wings and feet: one for soaring and the other for serving. *Both are essential.* When one dominates, there is spiritual imbalance.

A couple trained at this Bible college heard that several destitute students had been eating nothing but oatmeal for four days. The couple first decided to pray for them. Then, remembering "Wings and Feet," they bought a quarter of beef, some vegetables and fruit and had them delivered anonymously to the students as they continued their prayers.

Lorna's problem brought me into "Wings and Feet." She was born with a large birthmark on her left cheek. It was dark brown, almost black, and covered with thick, velvety-looking hair. Year after year, she looked in the mirror every night while brushing her teeth before bedtime and prayed that Jesus would take it away while she slept.

Children can be so cruel. Some of them nicknamed her, "Leech Face." Lorna was seventeen the first time I saw her. I noticed that she pulled her hair over, trying to hide the birthmark. This moved me deeply, and I said, "How thankful I am that my daughters don't have such a terrible handicap!"

The second time I saw her, I was touched when she sang in a very sweet voice. I went home and prayed, "Oh Jesus, our great physician, please take that thing away."

The third time I saw her, I drove home silently in the car with my family, and suddenly, as though someone had flipped on a light switch in a dark room, I felt a strong inner urge: "You've prayed. Now do something."

The following morning I called a skin specialist and plastic surgeon in the largest city near us. He agreed to see her. Realizing that I couldn't help financially, I contacted a wealthy couple in Texas who have no children. They agreed to pay the medical bills if they could remain anonymous.

After two surgeries and months of healing, Lorna's face was normal—and beautiful. It was a joy to hear her sing, and to watch her play basketball with a new poise and special lilt to her personality. The anonymous donors in Texas have a picture of her, before and after, and quietly rejoice. My role was to pray and make several telephone calls.

Wings and feet—what a great combination!

I wondered—could this blending of super and natural fulfill one at any age, in any walk of life? I continued my search for more answers.

5

OUR DREAMS WILL GUIDE US

IN THEIR EAGERNESS to grow in faith, to become closer to God, many today yearn for miraculous signs and wonders. They want their encounters with God to be like Paul's on the Damascus Road. Or to have visions like the Old Testament prophets. Or healings like the ten lepers.

Such miraculous experiences are happening today to a few; but God is regularly appearing to the many in more natural ways, which we overlook. Sometimes He speaks in our dreams.

These nightly events seem so commonplace that we don't see God in them. If God actually appeared in one of our dreams, or clearly spoke to us, we would pay attention. Since most dreams are vague, we usually make no effort to try and understand them or see any message in them for ourselves.

In recent years my attitude has changed toward dreams. I'm convinced that God will use our dreams to warn us about dangers ahead, guide us in making decisions, and reassure us of His Fatherly love.

One who received a warning was Debbie Demaree. She and her husband, Dan, entertained me some months ago in their home in Morgantown, West Virginia. They are a couple in their twenties who are enjoying their decision to get back to basics. They dress comfortably, live frugally, avoid junk food, and feel it is in vogue to talk about God, worship, and prayer.

I felt at home in their small, rustic house, nestled in the deep woods along the slope overlooking the Cheat River. When we arrived, it was necessary to ask the cat to remove himself from the old wooden rocker on the balcony so we could sit and talk. We chatted about Dan's insurance business, his previous summer's job as a guide for white-water kyak racing and then came to Debbie's therapeutic dream.

Debbie is vivacious, with long, chestnut brown hair and a few matching freckles sprinkled across her small nose. I found it hard to believe that she had come through a severe testing time with her health. In March of 1979, she described herself as emotionally ill from trying to handle her own as well as everyone else's problems.

"I had become a prisoner of impressions," she said. "I was trying to impress and was straining to be impressed, all the while worried about what everyone else thought."

Being a surgical nurse, Debbie was driven by the urge to be thoroughly sure, to be the best in her field. She took great pride in her diagnostic ability and knowledge. But when fatigue, sleeplessness, inability to eat and a series of aches and pains wore her down, she was totally incapable of analyzing her own case. This went on for almost a year.

Before falling asleep one night, Dan and Debbie prayed that God would help by leading them to an analyst who could reveal her trouble. She described the dream that then occured:

> I was watching a fast-moving volleyball game. Both teams
> were good and doing well. But, on one team was a small midget-

sized player, an almost dwarf-like character, who was antagon-
izing the other members of his team by flitting from position to
position, trying to play everyone's position except his own. They
were all angry at him. Suddenly the ball landed in his position,
but he was not there. I strained to get a look at his face. That pesky
creature, the player, was me.

Debbie felt she knew what the dream was saying to her: she
was to quit trying to play God in other people's lives; she was
not to take herself so seriously; and she was to become a
servant to others. To be sure about her interpretation, she
shared the dream with a mature Christian friend. Then they
both prayed about it. Debbie was directed to the following
Scripture which she felt was the conclusion of the whole
matter: "Let every man abide in the same calling wherein he
was called. Brethren, let every man wherein he is called
therein abide with God" (I Corinthians 7:20, 24).

Or to use her modern paraphrase, "Play your own field."

Debbie reported that this one dream enabled her to
recapture her perspective about life and regain her mental
health because she knew it was a *direct, supernatural word of
correction* to her from the Lord.

Our son, Carl David, had a rare dream a few years ago,
which he shared with us in a letter. At this period he admitted
that life for him and his wife, Diane, had become staggeringly
complicated. They were shopping for a new home and, in
general, tasting the sweetness of success. Yet something was
wrong. He wasn't enjoying life as he used to. Why and how
had things gone awry?

One night after Diane and their two sons, Chris and Craig,
had fallen asleep, he prayed silently, "Lord, show me what's
wrong with everything. When did my joy drain away? Syn-
chronize me again with Your fine-tuning." Then he had this
dream:

I was sitting in the front seat of a magnificent automobile. I often found myself trying to assist and tell the driver how to drive, criticizing, even grabbing the wheel on occasions. Suddenly, the driver pulled to the side of the road and came to a quick, deliberate halt. He looked at me lovingly but firmly and said, 'You keep insisting that you must do the driving, but you cannot drive. I must steer. If you stubbornly continue as you are, then I will open the door and you must get out. I will leave you here alone on the road. The choice is yours. You can walk alone, slowly, or ride swiftly and surely with me!

Carl David said the dream startled him and he let it settle for a few days before trying to understand it fully. Then while he was praying one morning, it all became clear to him—like a glass of muddy water when the sediment settles to the bottom. The Lord was showing Carl David that He was Boss and only when he accepted this would life regain its savor.

Since this dream revelation, Carl David and Diane have restructured their home life to put God first in everything.

On occasion, I believe, God gives us a prophetic dream which we can hold on to as a promise. This happened once in my marriage to John Upchurch. During the first year of our marriage I realized that because of a religious difference in our backgrounds, John had decided not to go to church. He had concluded that if he went to church with me, he would offend his mother and if he went to his mother's church he would offend me, so he went to neither. It was a handicap to our blending and unity.

After discussing it, we both decided to "live and let live." But I prayed earnestly for John to be drawn closer to me and to God and the church. Then I had this dream:

I was looking at a very large frame made of maple wood. In it was a fine-quality oil painting. Viewing it closely, I saw that it

was a portrait of John. He had both hands raised in worship with
a very tranquil, yet ecstatic look on his face.

When I awakened, I was suddenly hopeful, and each Sunday from then on I anticipated his coming to church with me.

But it did not happen. Then John was drafted into the U.S. Army and left for Fort Hood, Texas. I doubted that the dream would ever come true.

While John was in service, I worked in a local jewelry store. Each noon I went home for lunch. One day as I sat to eat, bowing my head to say grace, I was holding on to that picture in my dream of John's ecstatic face in worship. At once came an assurance — a vision perhaps — that was even more vivid than the original dream. I saw John and me in the act of going to church together. As confirmation, when I read the Scripture message that day in my devotional guide it was, "Never doubt in the dark, what God has told you in the light."

The weekend after John was discharged from the Army, months after my dream, he announced that he would attend church with me. At the close of the service, I was sitting with my head bowed, eyes closed while the minister invited those who wanted to accept Jesus and go forward. When I looked up John was no longer beside me. He was kneeling at the altar so that I had a full view of his face; his hands were raised in worship and there was that tranquil yet ecstatic facial expression — exactly as I had seen him in my dream years before.

Several weeks ago, I received a phone call from a distraught couple in their thirties, whose twelve-year-old daughter suddenly and unexpectedly died. Being Christians, they believed in life after death and they prayed on the way to the hospital, "Not my will but thine be done." Still they questioned. Why death for such a young and lovely child?

Despite the comfort supplied by their family and friends,

this young couple continued to hurt. Bitterness was creeping in—until the Lord spoke to the husband in a surprising way.

One night he couldn't sleep. He slipped out of bed and went into their guest room where he began reading in the book of Job. He read the account where it said, "The Lord gave Job twice as much as he had before" (Job 42:10). It was some comfort to him that Job, a perfect man, had his troubles, too, and that God had spoken to Job in his affliction. But he was not satisfied.

He describes his actions after putting his Bible down as being like a spoiled child: "I knelt beside the bed, beating my chest in remorse and even anger at God, questioning why, and begging foolishly, 'Bring her back to me.'" Then he fell asleep and had this dream:

> I was walking up a velvety-textured, green hill, beating my chest, crying, "God, send her back." When I approached a big city, a gate was opened to me. I pleaded, "Let me take her home with me."
>
> Gently but firmly, a very strong, tall Being reached down and lifted me, for I had fallen on my face. Taking a long, white soft handkerchief, this Person wiped my tears away and instructed me, "Yes, I'll let you take her back if you will promise me that you will never embarrass her, and you will keep her from hurts. Promise me that she will not become the victim of drugs, and that she will never be raped. That when she is turning gray with age, she will not suffer the tormenting pain of rheumatoid arthritis."
>
> "I cannot promise those things," I replied.
>
> "Then read this and be comforted." The Divine Being then handed me an open book with a marked passage. I looked, and read Isaiah 57:1, "The good are taken away from the evil to come."

Since I'm no expert on the subject of dreams, I've gone to one who is for some help in their interpretation. Dr. Herman Riffel (Your Dreams: God's Neglected Gift) offers these guidelines:

1. Believe that God uses dreams as one way of communicating to His people.

2. Keep a note pad and pencil by your bed so that you can write down the details of your dream as soon as you awake.

3. The interpretation of some dreams is fairly obvious; most are not since dreams are full of symbols which need to be understood in order to find the right interpretation.

4. Never act on the basis of a dream without checking it with both a mature believer and someone knowledgeable in dream interpretation, and never act on a dream that would go against anything in holy Scripture.

The dream is such a natural regular happening we tend to ignore it. And since we all tend to get too busy during the day to listen to Him, God takes what is natural in our sleep, adds His super touch—the dream—and speaks through it to us of important things.

6

COURAGE TO LIVE

IN MY PROBING to uncover the secrets of blending the super and the natural, I kept looking afar for exciting examples. I was eager to explore some of man's great acts of courage. Down through history, there certainly have been indomitable acts of heroism where faith in God has given people an overdrive of spiritual power. How did it happen?

God quietly suggested that there were answers closer to home—in our own backyard. How could that be? I questioned. We were such ordinary people.

Yet it was in just such an unlikely place, through one of God's supposedly lower creations, that I discovered one of the truths I had been seeking.

It all began one day in May, which is early spring in the Dakotas. Our three Collie dogs were running in the fields, jubilant over the first whiff of warmer weather. They chased a rabbit along the creek bed and through the orchard. From my bedroom window, I saw them cross the road and hoped that traffic was light and moving slowly.

Late that afternoon, April and I had taken a drive out behind the hills at back of our property. Since Carl was out of town, we leisurely drank in the beauty of the greening countryside, and decided that dinner could be late. When we turned into the driveway at home, we noticed a car stopped in the middle of the road in front of our mail box. A family was bending over an object in the road.

A pang shot through me. *Not one of our . . .*

"I had no choice. They were right in front of me. I swerved but couldn't miss all of them." The young woman speaking to us had a forlorn, crushed look on her face.

"Oh no, not Missy!" Fearfully, April and I bent over the Collie we called "Mother Superior." The other two dogs were loved, too, but Missy had been with us for almost ten years. She was family—a gentle, loving animal with human qualities.

April, then nine, dropped on her knees sobbing and wiped the blood from Old Missy's mouth and nose with her blouse sleeve. "Old Miss, don't die. Please get up, Old Miss. Come on, pretty girl, come on," she begged.

Hurt swelled up inside me, so large it crowded my lungs. My throat was swollen like cement until my temples pumped and my tear ducts were clogged. I couldn't even cry, I was so hurt.

The three of us rushed into our house. While the lady driver phoned the veterinarian to say we were coming, April and I removed the pink, linen tablecloth from the dining room table and ran back to Missy. We slid the tablecloth under her beautiful but limp sable and white, furry body. The back part of her body was flattened, having been dragged under the wheels of the skidding car. As we placed her gently on the front seat of the car, Missy raised her head, and with those sad, brown Collie eyes, she pleaded for help. Her faint, painful whine was almost more than we could take.

As we slowly drove the two miles to the veterinarian, I remembered how proud we were of Misty Lady of

Whispering Pines. I recalled the day we got her and that we had registered her with the American Kennel Club. She was of the Bellehaven strain and bloodline, and a descendant of one of the Lassies in the television series. There had been six Lassies altogether, and Missy was of the lineage of the second.

We had bought Missy before April was born. I remembered what happened when we brought April home from the hospital, at three days old. Missy greeted us, smelled the new pink shawl and, when we placed the baby in the bassinet, immediately appointed herself "guardian angel." She would lie beside her new charge day and night. One afternoon, a man who lived nearby came with a gift for the new baby. When he touched the doorknob of April's room, Missy grabbed his sleeve firmly in her teeth and held him there until I appeared to invite the man inside.

When April began toddling about, she would occasionally fall down. Quickly Missy would appear and grasping April's clothing at her back, gently lift the child to her feet. If April's diapers needed changing, Missy would sniff, bark and come to me. If I didn't respond, she would bark again, return to the baby, then to me, sniffing and barking until I did my motherly duty. She was a natural baby-sitter.

When April grew a little older and wandered too far from the house, Missy would tattle on her by coming to the front door barking, and then returning to April to warn and admonish the child with more barking.

After John's death, we were never afraid at night, even without a daddy and husband, because Missy was a sensitive, attentive protector of our household.

I'll never forget the day Missy nearly ripped the screen off the patio enclosure. Endeavoring to gain my attention, Missy was barking and running back and forth between the patio and April's jumpchair. I thought she was angry because April was perhaps playing too roughly with one of the puppies. When I investigated, however, I found a small diamondback rattlesnake coiled near both the puppy and April. After snatching child and puppy from danger, my brother, Marvin, who was visiting us, dispatched the snake with a shovel.

As we turned into the driveway at the vet's clinic, I glanced at Missy. The bleeding had stopped from her nose and mouth, but she seemed lifeless. Her eyes were closed. Gently, April and I carried her into the veterinarian's receiving room.

A middle-aged man, leathery but with kind eyes, was seated beside an examining table on which we placed Missy. After pricking the pads of her feet, examining her ears and eyes, and checking the spinal column and back legs, the vet turned his attention to us. "Her eyes are beginning to refocus and she seems alert, but her spinal cord may be severed. Her whole rear section is paralyzed and she's in a lot of pain. Time will tell if her internal organs can function. She may not be able to eliminate at all."

He paused and stroked Missy's head. "She sure is beautiful and gentle in spite of her shock and suffering. It'll be a long road, but if you really love that dog—and if she were mine— I'd gamble for a little more time. We can always put her to sleep if she doesn't die on her own."

When the vet's wife and daughter appeared, they too were encouraging. The veterinarian had no hospital facilities to care for Missy, so it was up to us. April and I gently carried Missy back to the car. As I turned to thank the vet, I realized for the first time that he was paralyzed from the waist down. His wife and daughter were helping him close up the office. No wonder he responded so lovingly to Missy's condition.

Arriving home, we made a stretcher out of a still cardboard box, and carried Missy into the "mud room"—our utility room just off the kitchen. We stroked her head and tried to comfort her. Whenever we left her alone, we could hear the pitiful, breathy, sighing cries.

During the first night, Missy's cries stabbed both April and me. We got up from bed, put aspirin in some hamburger and tried to feed her. Missy's mouth was too sore and she could not open or swallow. We finally dissolved aspirin in warm water and with a spoon, pried her mouth open and, holding her head up and back, forced it to go down, relieving her suffering to some extent. In the days that followed, we fed her fluids—milk and broth—this same way, pouring it between her clenched teeth.

When Carl returned from his business trip, he too became involved in our life-saving effort. But sleepless nights soon took a toll on the family. Carl particularly needed a good night's sleep for work, but his tender heart and sympathetic nature would not let him drop off when Missy cried.

At the end of the first week, Carl and I talked it through and came to a practical decision. The next day, when April went to softball practice, we would take Missy to the vet's office and have her put to sleep. Then we would simply give April the honest report that Missy had died.

The time came and Carl looked at me helplessly. "I can't do it," he said. He couldn't put it into words. Missy's battle to live had gotten to him. This natural drive to survive is in all of us. With Missy there was something added.

We postponed having her put to sleep for one more day, then another.

One night, Carl carried Missy out to the barn and laid her in some soft hay so we would not hear her cries. He came back to bed, tossed and turned for an hour, then got up again and retrieved the Collie from the barn. "I couldn't leave her out there to suffer alone," he said quietly when he climbed back into bed for the second time.

But did it make sense to let Missy suffer so? And the odor of the suffering animal penetrated the whole house. We kept disposable diapers under her, and kept changing them, but still our visitors crinkled their noses and must have thought us crazy to do all this for a dog.

We prayed earnestly for Missy, knowing that a loving Father cared tenderly for all His creatures. Then before our eyes, prayer became real to April as she implored God to heal her beloved Collie. But we desperately needed some sign that the total disruption of our household and all-out focus on the severely wounded animal was not a silly, overly-sentimental, emotional binge.

The sign came one morning. The swelling in Missy's hind section went down enough for her to have normal bowel movement, though not without some difficulty.

Then began the battle with bed sores on her thin, bony hips. We turned her often, but the sores persisted. Next, we had to remove maggots from the wounds around the rectal area. Who was suffering more, the dog or the family?

One night Missy's moaning became so intense that Carl arose, put on his bathrobe and told me to try and sleep. "I'll try and quiet her." I did go to sleep and awoke as dawn was breaking. Carl had not returned. I tiptoed downstairs to a scene that will stay with me forever.

Carl was lying on the hard floor beside Missy. She was breathing deeply, peaceful in her first genuine sleep for many days, her head cradled in the palm of my husband's big left hand. She was sustained and comforted in the fact that she was not alone.

At this point, I knew that even if Missy's gorgeous tail and back legs rotted off (which the vet had indicated was possible), requiring amputation, we would still keep her and help her to enjoy whatever living was possible. For there was an indomitable quality in Missy's will to live, a supernatural courage that had permeated every member of our family. Through Missy we had grown closer together. We understood pain now, in its full dimension. We had gained a new insight about how the Lord must suffer for His wounded children.

Missy's recovery now began. Every day we took her outside and laid her in the soft, green grass. The other two dogs licked her face, sniffed her, jumped over her, then raced away, while Missy's sad eyes followed them as they frolicked.

We would leave her in the sun a while, then remove her into the tree's shade. We fed her by hand, and offered her water frequently. The months wore on into July and August. Every evening about dark, her bark (she had one again), told us that she wanted to come back into the shelter and safety of the mud room.

One morning, April got up early and decided to fix her own breakfast. But first she stepped to the door to say, "Good morning, Old Miss." From all the way in the bedroom I heard her shriek, "She wagged! I swear, she wagged her tail!"

Carl and I ran downstairs and looked at Missy who stared at us solemnly. But there was no movement in her rear parts. We suggested to April that it was her imagination. She denied this so vigorously that we decided on a new exercise program for the Collie.

We took a bed sheet and hung it from a low hanging limb on the apple tree beside the driveway. Tying one end around Missy's mid-section, we let her hang there for an hour every day, holding her in a standing position. Then we talked, coaxed and rubbed her feet and legs. Nothing happened.

When we put weight on her back legs, she hopelessly flopped down to the ground like a limp, wet towel. Our hearts broke as we watched Missy struggle to pull her flat posterior around using the swimming motion of her strong front legs. Some people thought us cruel to push her so hard, for there was no hair on her right back hip and leg. But we were encouraged, for she was sleeping and no longer crying. Such courage! Still the question remained: would she move about better if we amputated her tail and rear legs?

Again we waited, and were rewarded. One day Missy pulled herself up on all four legs using the back ones like two crutches. After a while they would collapse, but Missy would get up again and again. Each time she did, we applauded and sang her praises.

Then one day we all saw it! She wagged her tail! After nearly five long, long months.

One September morning, April had just gotten on the school bus and Carl was making some phone calls from his study in the house. I looked out the back window and saw the gorgeous sight of our neighbor's sunflower fields in full bloom, yellow heads facing the morning sun. We had been so involved in the duties at hand, besides Missy's recuperation and the endless hours of attention required, we had not been aware of this beauty bursting forth at our own back door.

I filled a large coffee mug to the brim, and started walking slowly, taking "eye pictures" along the small lake nearby between our property line and our neighbor's. Then I stopped about two rows into the yellow sea of sunflowers to absorb the color, the scene, the fresh air and God's morning. I had been there several minutes when I heard a shuffling, swishing, scraping sound behind me. Turning I thought what I saw was a mirage in the bright sun. But it was reality! Here she came, struggling, dragging, but surely—with all the persistence and tenacity she could muster—Misty Lady of Whispering Pines had followed me.

I average crying about once every two years, whether I need to or not. On this beautiful morning I dropped on my knees between those sunflower rows and, burying my face in Missy's soft, white, furry shawl, I wept and thanked God.

She could not walk back since she had used the last ounce of her strength to get there. I carried her back home and arrived out of breath, but mustered a scream that brought Carl running from the house. Together we stroked her and loved her, tears running down our faces.

Later, April and I took Missy to the vet. He made her a pair of makeshift boot-shoes out of stiff plastic. Each morning thereafter we put them on her back feet to support her ankles and keep her feet pointing forward. The shoes were removed at night. Soon Missy began to run and play with the other dogs. It was not long until she became so active that the boots became tangled with weeds and burrs. Then we discarded them.

Missy always had a slight stiffness in her legs, but her hair grew back and the tail became bushy and wagged again. She lived a long time after that and finally died peacefully of old age.

What a legacy she left us! We saw again how God gives us something very basic and natural—the will to survive. Then when we go to Him for extra strength, He provides it, enriching us in other ways as well.

For we emerged from Missy's ordeal, a closer family, a stronger family, a more loving family.

7

WHEN GOD SAYS, "WAIT."

How OFTEN I mess up things because I want something now, quickly, when just a bit of patience would have saved the situation. "Why am I this way, Lord?" I keep asking. "Is the 'hurry up and do it now' syndrome something you built into all of us?"

The answer I keep getting is that the Lord honors the doers of this world. He blesses those who move ahead precipitously into difficult situations; I sense that He always prefers the impulsive ones over the timid and hesitant. That's why He loved King David so much.

But I'm also convinced that those who tend to act quickly and impulsively are not in God's perfect will. Our natural drives and desires may be God-given, and He honors them, but I've concluded that He is always trying to give us His better plan — a super natural way of dealing with life's most important decisions and confrontations.

Although we say we want God's timing for the key events of our lives, it is hard for us to trust Him and believe that His plan for us can be so much better than the one we are anxiously trying to work out in our own wisdom.

The story of Nate Lewis* illustrates this better than any I know.

Nate was a kind of "boy wonder," a man in a hurry who had his own successful construction firm when he was thirty. He is tall, blond, of Danish ancestry and has always had an unusual gift of persuading other people to do what he wants them to do. Not that Nate was completely self-centered. He joined a Lutheran church, gave generously to it and to other worthy causes. But Nate was always in control of his life.

When he met the very beautiful Sharon Jones, Nate decided instantly that this was the girl he wanted to marry. Sharon was from an affluent family, willful and impetuous like himself, and a young woman who loved to champion far-out causes. As they dated, Sharon was quite honest with Nate about herself. At the close of one evening together, she side-stepped his affectionate grasp and faced him head on.

"Nate, you say you're in love with me, but you don't know me. I'm not interested in marriage—I detest housekeeping, can't cook and do not want to bear children. In fact, even the thought of caring for children makes me feel like a Russian peasant."

Nate was a bit shocked by this, yet he found Sharon's independent manner and tall, statuesque figure deeply desirable. He decided that Sharon was putting up resistance to test him. She could change, *would* change after marrying him. So he pursued her more ardently. And won her.

But after months of marriage, Sharon did not change. She became moody and restless. If he hadn't hired a full-time cook and maid, their household would have been a disaster area. Even harder for Nate was her indifference to his love-making.

* All names have been changed.

In spite of their incompatibility, a daughter was born, then a son. Both were cared for by a nurse. Sharon had resumed activity in some of her far-out causes, to Nate's dismay. They argued loudly and often.

"You never have understood me," Sharon snapped at him one night. "You think of a wife as a possession, someone who will stroke you and admire you and jump when you call. I'm not that kind of a female."

"What kind are you then?" Nate shot back.

Sharon hesitated. "Different. I have different likes and desires than you have. I tried to tell you this before we married. You wouldn't hear me. You knew better. You sold me on the idea that marriage to you would be more exciting than the life I was living as a single. It has not turned out that way."

Nate ground his teeth in frustration. "What is it you want, Sharon?"

"More freedom to go places and do things on my own."

"I don't want you getting involved again with your old crowd," Nate said grimly. "Some of them are real weirdos."

Sharon grew icy. "Did it ever occur to you that they feel the same way about you?"

A hot argument followed. Nate gave in partially. He didn't object when Sharon said she wanted to fly to the West Coast with a woman friend to attend a celebrity golf tournament.

Sharon returned to their plush suburban home five days later and locked herself in the separate bedroom she had been using for some months. Only when Nate threatened to break in the door did she open it. Nate was in for a severe shock.

Sharon had been badly beaten. One eye was swollen almost shut. There were red welts on her face and neck. A nasty cut ran along the side of one cheek. When Nate insisted on examining the rest of her body, he found more scratches and bruises.

Stunned, he demanded an explanation. She refused and would say nothing more. Nate then tried to reach Shirley, the

woman friend she'd travelled with. It took him almost a week
to track her down. When he finally reached her by phone, she
was noncommittal. Only when Nate threatened to bring the
police into the situation, she relented.

"All right, Nate, I guess it has to come out sooner or later.
Sharon and I had a fight."

"Over what? You should see her, Shirley. She's beat up
terribly."

"I'm sorry." There was sobbing at the other end of the
phone.

"I had too much to drink one night. We quarrelled and ..."

"I just don't understand, Shirley." Nate was angry and
frustrated. "How could you do this to a friend?"

"You might as well know, Nate. Sharon and I are more
than friends. We've been lovers for many years. But I've
found someone else recently. Sharon didn't like it when I told
her. She came at me with her fists and it was a bloody battle."

Nate hung up in a state of numbed bewilderment.
Sharon—a lesbian all these years? How could such a beautiful woman go that route? How could she do this to him? No
wonder she had avoided his love-making.

For days he walked about the house and roamed the nearby
fields, thinking and really praying for the first time in his life.
At long last he was faced with a problem out of his control.
He loved his wife despite her bizarre unfaithfulness. He did
not want to dissolve the marriage even though he knew
Sharon would quickly agree to a divorce. Their two young
children needed their mother.

It was a week before Sharon came out of her room. She
sought Nate in his den and spoke with her usual bluntness.
"You called Shirley, didn't you?"

"Yes."

"What did she tell you?"

"The whole story."

Sharon winced only momentarily. "Do you want a
divorce?"

"No."

"You can have it any time you want. And the children too."

Nate's voice was soft. "I don't want to break up our home. I still love you and want us to try and make our marriage work."

For the first time Sharon lost her composure and tears glistened in her eyes. Then she pulled herself together. "It'll never work, Nate."

"Will you try again?"

"Yes, I'll try again."

Sharon did make an effort. They began attending church together and Sharon even went for several sessions of counseling with their quiet-spoken, gray-haired pastor. She asked for understanding, but refused to pray for change. Then Nate decided to move his business to a smaller town 150 miles away to give them a new start and to get Sharon farther away from old friends.

The children were now three and five and delightful. But nothing inside of Sharon had changed. She hated the new town, was bored with her house and family, and missed her old friends and haunts. She went back for a day's visit and stayed a week.

Nate was angry about it; Sharon was defiant. A new and worse confrontation occurred. Then, when Nate was away on a business trip, Sharon packed her things and moved out.

When Nate discovered that his wife had settled in with a new lover—another woman—something gave inside of him. He made no effort to contact her. He ignored his business for days at a time. Most of his employees knew of the separation—and one young woman indicated her availability to help him forget.

Out of desperation, he sought his former pastor and told him the whole story. The gray-haired man was kind but blunt. "You've always gotten what you wanted in life, Nate. Jesus Christ has never been more than an afterthought to you. Now you really do need Him. I can't help you, but He can. I honestly believe that Jesus is your only hope in this situation."

Nate left the pastor frustrated. The "come to Jesus" approach had always seemed simplistic and embarrassingly emotional. He believed in God, went to church, gave to Christian causes. That did it as far as he was concerned.

After the children were in bed, he wandered restlessly about the house. The aloneness was too much. He would seek out that woman in his office. Anything was better than living alone with his misery over Sharon.

Then suddenly he found himself on his knees by his bed. "Lord, where are you? Jesus, if you're for real, help me." Nate found himself flinging out his right hand imperiously as though hailing a taxi in the heart of a city.

Then something broke inside him and the tears gushed forth. Nate had not cried like this since he was a boy. The demanding tone was suddenly gone. "Jesus, I'm desperate. I can't do it on my own any longer. I want You in my life. That's right, Jesus, I'll say it again more clearly. I want you to run my life."

I'm not sure what Nate expected to happen at that point. I don't think he knew what to expect. But a significant change had occurred inside him. He had abdicated his throne, stopped playing God, and surrendered this role to the Lord God Almighty. A new relationship was begun. Then through his pastor he was led to several Christian businessmen who helped him begin his new life.

Through these people Nate received a clear word from the Lord. He was to develop his new relationship with Jesus— and wait. Yes, wait.

For such a supreme activist as Nate, this seemed not only excruciating punishment, but a kind of verification of his former criticism of religious people as pious do-nothings.

"Not so," he was told firmly. *Waiting on the Lord* was one of the most difficult, and highest forms of faith. To such a high achiever as Nate Lewis, the Lord had presented one of the most difficult of challenges. Then he was asked to comb his Bible for all the references he could find on the subject of waiting.

"But what am I to wait for?" asked the practical-minded Nate.

"For the Lord to work out His plan for your life," came the answer.

Nate shook his head. "That sounds like I'm to go off somewhere and just hibernate. I can't just do nothing."

"You're not supposed to stop your normal activities. You have a father's role with your children and a business to run. Keep active, but don't force new situations on your family or business until you get clear guidance from the Lord."

It seemed terribly vague to Nate, but he followed the advice as best he could. He looked up the subject in a concordance and stopped counting after coming up with twenty-five separate references in Scripture on "wait upon the Lord." This was sobering. So much emphasis in the Bible had to mean it was important.

On several occasions, Nate was tempted to have an affair as a way of lashing out against his unfaithful wife. Something stopped him. After one sleepless night he decided he would go ahead and divorce Sharon. She expected it. And his pride was really suffering. Later that day he changed his mind and decided to wait.

Meanwhile Nate realized that something was different inside him. The pressure was gone. He felt cleaner than ever before in his life. He was glad he hadn't started an affair or divorce proceedings. He spent longer periods with his children.

Months passed. At times Nate had to resist the old urges to take charge of things, to force a confrontation with Sharon, to get on with a new life. The word continued to be *wait.*

Then one day Sharon came home. She called first to ask if it was all right. Nate assured her it was. She had lost weight and looked tired and drawn. Her eyes were listless. As always, she was honest.

"It didn't work out," she said wearily. "I hate myself for coming back this way, but I've nowhere else to go. Besides I feel just lousy, and I'm not ready or able to resume being a wife. May I have my old room?"

Nate found himself seeing Sharon for the first time as she really was—a confused, selfish, maverick person. He felt compassion for her, then realized he no longer loved her. This love had somehow been removed from him. *How extraordinary*, he mused.

When Sharon began having fainting spells, Nate took her to the hospital for tests. Exploratory surgery was done. The findings: cancer of the stomach, liver and colon—in the final stages. Her condition was so bad, doctors would not even let her go home.

Shocked, Nate obtained the services of a professional nurse to give Sharon personal attention. He was allowed to bring the children in for short visits, after which he turned them over to this special duty nurse who entertained them in the waiting room while he sat by his wife's bed.

Sharon lived only two more weeks. During that time Nate tried hard to persuade his wife to make the same kind of commitment to Jesus Christ that he had done. She was stubbornly resistant. "You and the nurse are ganging up on me," she complained bitterly.

"What nurse?" Nate asked in surprise.

"That one you hired."

"I didn't even know she was a Christian."

"Well, tell her to lay off."

Nate found the nurse and his two children giggling together in a corner of the waiting room as she read to them from a picture book. For the first time, he really looked at her. Her name was Mabel Stevens. She was youngish—probably about thirty—with warm laughing brown eyes, firm chin, and of medium height. For once he felt slightly at a loss for words. He couldn't talk frankly to her in front of the children.

"I appreciate your concern for my wife," he began a bit lamely.

"Thank you. She's hurting in so many ways."

"I know. She resists our talking about the Lord."

"Yes." Nurse Stevens was silent a moment. "Should I stop trying?"

"No—er—I think we should, well, make the effort. I'd like to talk to you alone about her sometime."

"I would like that."

While driving the children home he asked them about Nurse Stevens. The response was enthusiastic. "We like her!"

Mabel Stevens was also a person who didn't like to wait. She had grown up with two big dreams: inspired by the story of Florence Nightingale, she decided as a young girl that she wanted to be a nurse; and she yearned to be a wife and mother.

After only one year of college, she left to become a nurse. But her hospital experience had been disheartening. Because of her quick mind and bright personality, she was moved into administrative work. Seldom did she minister to patients. Soon she found herself having to resist deceptive medical practices by other nurses and doctors. She quit her job and became an independent professional nurse, available only for special jobs like the one with Sharon.

Mabel's second dream now seemed dead, too. An operation several years before had seen to that. It was supposed to have corrected a menstrual problem. The doctor had botched it, and then a hysterectomy was done.

This had resulted in a real confrontation between Mabel and her Lord. "Why? Why?" she had wailed, when she learned that her dream of motherhood was ended. For months, she brooded and sulked, feeding her self-pity. Then one night in a state of bewildered agony, she had poured out all her frustration to God. Strangely, peace had followed. She felt comforted, assured. Her dreams had not been crushed. She was to *wait*.

Waiting was easier for Mabel than for Nate. Perhaps it's easier for women. The months passed. There had been several young men on the scene. Two she had particularly liked, both medical interns. Both had been attracted to Mable, but their goals had been different — very materialistic. They also wanted an intimate relationship without marriage, without commitment. Sadly, Mabel turned them down.

When she first saw Nate Lewis walk into Sharon's hospital room with his two dear little children, her heart had pounded wildly. He barely noticed her, so upset was he over his wife's condition. And rightly so. "But why, Lord, did something stir so strongly in my heart?" she prayed later that evening when she came home from the hospital.

Then before bedtime while reading her Bible, one verse totally captured her attention. "All that the Father giveth me shall come to me" (John 6:37).

She read it again, paraphrased it this way: "That which is mine will come if I patiently wait."

The timing seemed significant. Could it have anything to do with Nate Lewis and his dying wife? The one thing she could certainly do was try and make Sharon's last days as pleasant as possible. It then came to Mabel that she should do all she could to bring Sharon to the Lord during her last hours.

On Nate's next visit to the hospital he came alone. Before leaving, he took Nurse Stevens to the waiting room for a firm talk about her evangelizing efforts toward Sharon. He wasn't sure he wanted this coming from a nurse.

Mabel totally disarmed him with her warm good humor and compassionate spirit. They agreed to pray separately for Sharon and hope for an opening from her. The rest of their conversation was about the two children, whom Mabel obviously adored.

A week later Sharon died. When Nate arrived at the hospital, Mabel met him outside the door of his wife's room with words of sympathy. "I'm sorry to report that Sharon resisted the Lord to the very end. Is there any way I can help with the children?" she asked.

"Yes. I would really like that," Nate answered.

In the months that followed a solid relationship of respect developed between Nate and Mabel. When Nate asked her to be a live-in nurse for the children, Mabel prayed about this and felt the Lord was still saying, *"Wait."* She continued to come for several hours each day to take care of the children's special needs. More and more Nate asked her to stay for dinner and on into the evening to discuss his activities.

The day finally came when Nate realized he loved Mabel, that she had become indispensable to him. He proposed marriage. She accepted. Today they are an admired couple, conscientious parents, all-out in their love for each other and the Lord, leaders in community activities.

A heartwarming, true story. And also a story with an important message for those people who are in such a hurry to live their lives to the utmost. The Lord has something so much better for you if you will only listen to Him—and *wait* for Him.

Nate did not rush into an affair that tempted him—and as a result he was emotionally ready for Mabel, the woman God always had in mind for him. He didn't divorce Sharon—he waited, and saved himself and his family from an ugly episode.

Mabel was tempted on several occasions to live with a medical student. Resisting this immediate gratification of her needs made her available for something so much better. Then later on, if she had moved into Nate's house as a nurse and housekeeper, she might well have remained in that capacity—and never become his wife.

We have a sovereign and loving Lord, who gives us freedom to go our own way, do our own thing and be as impulsive as we wish in this beautiful world He created. He can and will overrule many of our mistakes. And always, He waits patiently for us, hoping we will see that pursuing our natural instincts and desires is being only half-alive. What He has to add to this—when the time is right—is so much better.

8

HOLY LAUGHTER

MY SEARCH FOR a new understanding of the *supernatural* had shown me over and over again that it is a word of two parts. God has given us the *natural* to enjoy, and He expects us to find Him there. And I do. I see Him every day in the natural beauty of my garden, in the dazzling brightness of nearby Clear Lake and in the loving, trusting eyes of our animals.

These natural things are good because they were created by God. But the natural is not the best unless He touches it with that *super* part of Himself. This happens when He personally enters our world, and He involves Himself with us and His Spirit—even enters into us.

I have tried to point out the different manifestations of super natural living—in our work, in family living, in worship, in our dreams, yes, in nearly every aspect of our life.

Even in our laughter.

One day I came across the phrase, *holy laughter*. This was a fresh thought! What exactly did it mean?

The Bible had some clues. In all the life that God created,

only to man and woman did He give the gift of laughter. Obviously He meant it to be used joyfully.

Scripture seems to confirm this: "A merry heart doeth good like medicine" (Proverbs 17:22). Does this mean there are healing qualities in laughter?

My brother, Gary, was visiting us a few years ago and awoke one day suffering from a migraine headache. He was still in great discomfort when we left the house—all dressed up— to go out to dinner. Walking out to the car suddenly I slipped in my high heels on a Collie-sized dog deposit. Sliding forward on my hands, I flopped on all fours into the manure.

There were exclamations of concern that I might be hurt. I wasn't. But my clothes were a mess. Suddenly I started to laugh and continued until my stomach hurt and tears rolled down my face. Gary, too, roared with uncontrollable laughter.

As he helped me up and back into the house to change clothes, he said with surprise, "My headache's gone!" Nor did it come back the rest of the day. The healing power of laughter!

A stockbroker who could not sleep rented funny film strips to show on his home projector before bedtime. He had discovered that ten minutes of genuine laughter induced about two hours of sound sleep.

I read of the thirteen-year-old boy, lying comatose in a hospital bed from a wound in the head. One afternoon, two nurses were in his room checking his charts and observing his unconscious condition. Something funny struck them and they began to laugh. To their stunned surprise, the unconscious boy laughed, too. Two days later, the boy was so improved he was removed from intensive care into a private room.

The healing quality in laughter must go deep into the heart and emotions and, in some way, stimulate fluids that cleanse

and purify the body. Doctors practicing "holistic" medicine
are making new discoveries in this area daily.

But is this the same as holy laughter? It seems to be close,
but the pratfall which produces laughter that heals a headache doesn't seem to fit, does it?

A story concerning my paternal grandfather, William
Perkins, gets us closer to the answer. Dad Perkins was a
school teacher with a scientific approach to life. He was not a
believer in much of anything. In fact, the thing he seemed to
love most in life was that pipe he kept clenched between his
teeth.

During a visit to our home, my mother and father once
invited him to one of our church services. The people at this
church were friendly and effervescent, radiating a kind of
spiritual joy. My parents hoped it would rub off on Dad Perky.
At the close of his sermon, the minister invited those who
wanted to receive Jesus as Lord and Savior to come forward
and kneel for prayer.

My grandfather did not even bow his head. He watched
stonily as a man from the back of the church got up and
walked down the aisle and knelt. My mother drew in her
breath in surprise, and whispered to Dad Perky that this man
had been in prison for many years after killing a man when
revenue agents raided his bootlegging operations. He had
only recently been paroled. In the community he was known
as a murderer, alcoholic and an outcast of society.

When the former convict knelt at the altar, several men
came from the audience and knelt beside him while the pastor
placed a loving arm around him as they prayed quietly. The
congregation was silent, solemn.

Suddenly there was something almost like a chemical
explosion. The kneeling man lifted his head and gripped the
altar as he let loose with a burst of laughter. It was joyous
laughter—rippling, happy, a contagious sound that spread
throughout the congregation. People began to smile, then

chuckle. It was a holy moment as a man who had been bound in sin most of his life found release.

In the car returning home, my mother and father wondered what Dad Perky's reaction had been. They didn't have long to wait. "Well, I paid a dollar to see your show, and I got my dollar's worth." (He had put a dollar in the offering plate.) "But I sure didn't see anything funny there at the end."

My father tried to explain that laughter was the loosening force in the man which God had used to free him from his past.

My grandfather shook his head. "Maybe so, but one time in your church is enough for me."

My folks were disappointed, for they felt that he too needed this kind of release. Though a brilliant man, a hard worker and a good provider for his family, Dad Perkins was basically joyless, depressed and unhappy.

But something was working inside my grandfather. On his next visit, he again went to church with us, and when the altar call was given, he went forward. His time of prayer was not a dramatic one like the former criminal's, but tranquil and peaceful as a soft, downy mist.

There were seven family members riding home from church that night in one car. A healing transformation had occurred in Grandfather. He was jolly and smiled at everything anyone said or did. And he did something I'll never forget. He put his pipe in his mouth and lit it. From the fire of the match I noticed that his eyes were twinkling.

Then he removed the pipe from his mouth, chuckling softly. Next he reached over me, rolled down the window and tossed the match out first, then the pipe.

"I won't need that thing any more," he said. "It was just a crutch to hide behind."

On December 2, 1967, Don and Dolores Smeeton, a newly married couple attending Evangel College in Springfield, Missouri, were involved in a serious automobile accident.

By the time the ambulance arrived at St. John's Hospital in Springfield, Missouri, there seemed little hope for Dolores' recovery. Although Don was badly hurt with a crushed jaw and a broken back, Dolores was even more seriously injured. Her face was completely mangled. According to her doctor, "the bones of her face were like glass bottles in a burlap bag smashed against a brick wall." First came a tracheotomy for breathing, then life-sustaining blood transfusions. The dangers were great—loss of brain fluid, risk of infection, possibility of brain damage.

A chain of prayer was set up, beginning with Dolores' parents who drove to the scene. As the word of the accident spread through the Smeetons' college community and through its students to many parts of the nation, the prayer chain grew. Numerous churches also took up the burden of prayer for the young couple. Two people—in separate states, not knowing why—were urged to pray for them at the exact time of the accident.

The crisis passed. A combination of prayer and the skill of her doctors saved her life. When Dolores did regain consciousness two days later, her first thoughts were, Where am I? Why can't I move? And then, *Why can't I see?*

After numerous tests, the verdict came: Dolores' blindness would be permanent. As the days, weeks and months of recuperation and adjustments began, both Don and Dolores found their faith put to the test.

Don's injuries healed fairly quickly. With Dolores, she found that even in her world of blackness, God remained. But the key to spiritual and mental health for both of them became the ability to laugh together. They decided to focus on that verse in Proverbs: "A merry heart doeth good like medicine: but a broken spirit drieth the bones."

The apparatus used on Dolores was a horseshoe-shaped halo around the forehead with wires piercing the skin to hold the bones so they could knit. One day, one of the screws worked itself loose causing the whole apparatus to shift slightly. As the doctor made his rounds that day, he was greeted by Dolores, who though in pain managed to quip, "Hey, doctor, can you help me? I have a screw loose."

On another occasion Don kidded her. "Look, Dolores, my broken back and jaw are *real* injuries. Yours are all in your head."

The day after Dolores was released from the hospital, she was back in class still wearing her metal halo. It was, she reminded her husband, the proof that she was an angel.

And so they learned to laugh together in their recuperation. While continuing her college work, she concluded, "It's not so bad being blind. You just have to be more organized." Through a course for the blind, she learned how to go anywhere alone with a white cane.

From these experiences, Dolores was able to say, "I am never alone. Jesus is with me. He is my Light and my Way. He has become my *Joy*. I no longer depend on the things I can see to make me happy."

People constantly wonder how it is possible for Dolores to travel independently around Chicago teaching other recently blinded adults. Or to care for her own household. Or to raise her two children. And, when her husband was transferred to Brussels, Belgium, to adjust to a new place and culture very different from her own.

She answers, "I don't live by sight, but by faith — and by touch, taste, smell and hearing."

The Smeetons have obviously shown great courage and faith to overcome tremendous physical and emotional wounds. When you are with them you have the feeling that there has been another essential, less recognized element in their recovery—their ability to laugh together over small things and big things. It's this kind of laughter that does a holy and healing work inside people.

Laughter, like prayer, can have a two-way effect. It can have a positive influence on those who hear it and be therapeutic to the one who is laughing. When God uses our laughter for His purposes, then it becomes holy.

Spencer Todd grew up in a state of rebellion. He was angry because his father had died when he was seven—an age when a boy is beginning to have a special need for a father. He resented his mother's marriage to another man a few years later, especially when he was then sent to a boarding school. He became a somber, unhappy teenager who seldom smiled. When he entered college, he tended to be a loner and had difficulty making friends.

On the campus of the university Spencer attended, there was a group of joyous Christians who met weekly for fellowship and prayer. In the early 1970s an explosion of the Holy Spirit took place at the university, largely sparked by this one group. Students began receiving something they called "the baptism of the Spirit," which resulted in joyous singing, hands raised in praise, speaking in tongues and even healings. University officials looked on in helpless disapproval. Since they allowed homosexual and atheistic groups to meet, they could hardly disapprove officially of this new burst of spirituality. What surprised Christian students the most was that some of the theology professors who had supported the granting of university facilities for the former groups, now viewed the Holy Spirit phenomena with stern disapproval.

Spencer Todd was invited to attend a prayer meeting and refused. Though his parents were Christians, and he had joined the church as a boy, he had resisted God ever since the death of his father. But two of the young Christian men persisted with Spencer until finally, "to get them off his back," he agreed to attend a meeting.

It was the music that first got through to Spencer. It was so joyous, so infectious that the somber young man began to join in despite his deep reserve. Then the quality of friendliness he found among the group was hard to resist. He came back again and again.

At the end of one meeting, the persistent young man who

had first approached Spencer came up to him with a wide grin.

"Spencer, I think it's time we prayed for you to receive the Holy Spirit."

"Why do you say that?" Spencer was already backing away mentally.

"Because you need Him. You're a closed-up person. Jesus wants to open you to His love and joy."

"I like the way I am now," Spencer replied stubbornly.

"Do you really?"

There was a long moment of silence. Spencer said later he stood there, knowing he was on a precipice, that a step forward would plunge him into the unknown. He was tired of his somber, lonely life, yet afraid of changing. But he was not given a chance to back away.

Spencer was surrounded by several grinning students who sat him in a nearby chair. A half-dozen laid hands on him and one began to pray:

"Lord Jesus, we pray for our friend Spencer, who has blocked You out of his life for many years. A thawing is taking place in him, Lord. Deep down he knows he needs You. He needs the love and joy You can give him. He wants this right now more than anything else in the world."

And Spencer reported later that at that point a deep hunger began forming inside him to receive the Lord. The walls of resistance he'd built around himself began to crumble.

The prayer continued: "Lord, we now ask You to come into Spencer's life with Your Spirit. Fill him up, Lord, with Yourself. Clean out all the sadness and unhappiness that has accumulated in Spencer. Replace it all with Your joy..."

It was then the laughter began. It started with a chuckle. Next, controlled giggling. Then Spencer's face lit up with one big smile and laughter exploded out of him. It went on and on and on....

It was as if all the walled-up sadness, sorrow, anger, resentment, self-pity and unhappiness had been scoured out of Spencer's insides and flushed up and out through peal after peal of laughter. It was not a raucous occasion but a holy time, for the laughter was mingled with tears.

Some of the students were surprised by Spencer's experience. Was this the way God sometimes baptized people with His Spirit?

The answer is a resounding, "Yes." This is the way God baptizes — and heals too.

Holy laughter is a blessed gift. When one receives it, he or she is truly enjoying the super natural life.

9

PROTECTION

As a teenager I was taught by my parents that those who committed their lives to Jesus Christ had obtained, by this act, a Friend, Counselor, Savior, Helper, Intercessor and Protector. I didn't understand then what all this meant because Jesus had not become that real to me.

Then an incident occurred that made me aware, perhaps for the first time, of the power He exercises as Protector in our world today.

I was baby-sitting with my little brothers in an antiquated manse house behind the church my father pastored in Mishawaka, Indiana. In the early evening, my dad had received a phone call to come to the emergency room of the hospital to pray for an auto-wreck victim. Mother was my dad's right arm in situations like this because of her gentle, but strong bedside manner. She rarely left us alone, but this was an emergency. I was then thirteen. As they left hurriedly, she told us, "Boys, you mind Betty. Betty, you're in charge. Be sweet to your brothers."

Soon after they left, I began to practice my accordion lesson when I heard a scream. It was coming from the bathroom — from my littlest brother, Jimmie, then eight years old. "Help, Betty!"

I threw open the door to the bathroom and gasped in horror. Jimmy was being pulled by his arms out the window located above the toilet bowl on which he had been sitting. The first sight that met me was my brother's bare bottom as it began to slide out the window. Then I saw a man's contorted face outside. All this flashed before me in less than a second.

I had no weapon, of course. I did the first thing that came to my mind, the only thing I had been taught to do. I screamed, "Jesus!"

The man reacted as if he had been shot. He dropped Jimmie and fled. My brother tumbled back into the bathroom, unhurt except for a small bruise on his rib cage.

The police were called by our next door neighbor. When my parents returned home, they were filled with frightened wonder at the crowd that had gathered on our front porch and the story I told them.

The morning South Bend Tribune carried the headline: FOIL ATTEMPT TO KIDNAP CHILD. We still have the copy as a reminder of the protection we receive when we call out the name of "Jesus."

The intruder was arrested the next day. He was a medical student in a nearby college, and had already been charged with slipping drugs from the lab, illegal possession of narcotics, peeping tom activity, and sexually molesting two small boys.

When we've told this story to friends over the years, some have questioned whether it was the word "Jesus" that so startled the intruder that he dropped Jimmie. "Wouldn't any alarmed cry from Betty have had the same effect?" they asked. "The natural reaction would be to panic and flee."

Perhaps so. Yet since that experience, I have heard of more

and more people* who have used the name of Jesus to obtain protection in times of danger. There is something beyond the natural that happens when we call upon His name.

A more recent experience confirmed this for me. This occurred with my step-daughter Connie several years after her father and I were married. Connie was then a senior in high school which was only one block from Trinity College where Carl taught.

On this particular afternoon, she had not come home directly after school. I was not bothered by this. Connie often went to see her father in his office, or would sit in on college classes in the late part of the day to enjoy those vibrant, college-age students.

I was preparing dinner, when suddenly a fear for Connie gripped me. For a moment I thought I would faint. Sometimes the alarm signal of fear for a certain person can be perception at a supernatural level. There can be two kinds of fear. One brings negative depression and *de*structive apprehension; the other is the *in*structive fear, which can be the Holy Spirit prompting you that there is an immediate need. In this case, it was the latter. I have learned to stop everything I am doing at such times and pray.

As I dropped to my knees at the kitchen chair, I noticed that it was ten minutes before 4:00 P.M. Laying my head on my arms, I called, "Jesus, please take care of Connie. She is in some kind of trouble. Protect her, Lord."

When I pray at times like this, I see the Son of God seizing a flaming sword and going forth to fight my battles. These words of my grandmother describe it:

"There is a place where Heaven's resistless power
    Responding, moves to your insistent plea;
There is a place, a silent, trusting hour

*See *Prayers That Are Answered* by Betty Malz

Where God descends and fights for you and me.
Where? It is the secret place of prayer."

When a feeling of peace came, I arose from my knees and
resumed dinner preparations. About 5:00 P.M., I heard soft
footsteps come in the front door. Glancing down the hallway,
I saw Connie quickly rushing up the stairs to her bedroom.
Her hair was dripping wet and her amber-colored corduroy
slacks were soaked. Then I heard the hair dryer running, and
a few minutes later she appeared in the kitchen with a cheery,
"What can I do to help?"

"You may set the table," I suggested, "but first tell me, was
anything wrong at ten minutes to four?"

She stared at me a moment, her eyes wide and startled.
Then with a sob, she rushed to me, threw her arms around
my neck and told me her story. A group of her friends had
decided that even though there was still some ice on the rim
of Elm Lake, the sun was so warm they would take a canoe
ride. An older student joining the group meanwhile, had
slipped some drinks to a few of the boys. The result was that
they had become "frisky." The canoe in which Connie and
some of the other girls were rowing was tipped over. She had
nearly drowned, struggling and swimming to shore through
the slushy, mushy, ice-water. Somehow she made it, she was
not sure how.

How important it was that I obeyed the impulse to pray for
Connie's protection! I realize we parents can be overly protective and make ourselves and our children miserably self-
conscious if we become too fearful. The other extreme is self-
centeredness which prevents us from being lovingly aware of
the dangers our children face, like one mother who told her
teenage son, "Don't tell me if you're taking drugs. I don't care
where you go, or when you come home at night. Just don't
wake me up to tell me. What I don't know won't hurt me."

Protection is a subject of huge importance today in our

violent world. Private protection agencies have mush-
roomed, their stock rising while other stocks are falling. All
police forces are overworked and undermanned. Govern-
ments are spending billions on armaments to protect their
land from aggressive neighbors. Huge amounts of money go
into protective measures against hijackers, kidnappers,
terrorists.

We live in a period of distrust. We double- or triple-bolt our
doors. Neighborhoods have set up crime watch programs and
have a special police number to dial when they see any
suspicious-looking people wandering about.

It is sad that we live in such an age, but it is the *natural* thing
to do to take such precautions. All I know of God tells me He
expects us to use our common sense in the matter of protection of lives and property.

But once again God has more to give us than the natural
things of this world which He created. There is that extra
dimension of His power through the Person of Jesus as our
Helper and Protector. We are told over and over again in
Scripture to call upon the name of Jesus. (See Luke 10:17;
John 14:13, 14; 16:23; Acts 16:18; Romans 10:13; Philippians
2:9, 10.)

There are many thousands — perhaps millions — of
parents who are praying today for the protection of their
children who have left homes to go into the world to make a
living. The most effective thing these parents can do for their
offspring is to pray. Words of advice at this stage seem to
have little impact.

One heartsick mother called me recently to say that she
and her husband had invested twenty-six years and most of
their earnings in their only daughter, Sandra, who had been
the joy of their lives. She had graduated from college with
honors, went into the Navy as a nurse and then developed a
drinking problem.

When Sandra was discharged from the service because of
her drinking, her parents were at a loss as to how they could

help her. Unfortunately they trusted her with two credit cards, hoping she would come home and resume working near them.

This did not happen. Sandra went off on her own, and ran up a debt of $6,000 on the credit cards. Sadly the parents had the credit cards cancelled, realizing that this might cut off all ties with their daughter. They asked me how to pray for Sandra, feeling that her drinking made her vulnerable to all kinds of dangers in the city where she lived.

After talking with Sandra's parents, I went off alone to pray, wishing that "Warhorse" Buckland, the greatest prayer warrior I ever knew, was still alive. Though a small, insignificant-looking woman, "Old Warhorse," as she was called, became a powerhouse when she began praying for others. I needed someone like her since it's always good, if possible, for two or more to be intercessors for the person in need. As my mind roamed over the mature, experienced people I knew, I picked up the phone and called Marge Block at the business where she is a secretary.

At one point in her life Marge had nearly lost her husband and home because of alcohol. God had set her free from that prison and restored to her all the things that alcohol had nearly separated from her. She would *know* how to pray, for she felt a call to help others with this problem. Quickly I outlined the situation to her on the telephone.

"Yes, I'll pray," Marge promised. "I'll lock my office and kneel and pray here while you pray at home, Betty. I can work overtime to make up for any time this takes away from my job."

When I knelt again, I felt this prayer reinforcement. The power of God was beginning to work for us. I tingled with the assurance that we had an audience with the Almighty.

A week or so later, I received a four-page letter from Sandra's mother. They had been pleasantly shocked to have their daughter suddenly appear at home. Immediately they noticed a personality change — her facial appearance was even different. At dinner that night, she told them of the strange experience she had just had.

"I was alone in the car, driving down a street 186 miles from home," Sandra told them. "It was late afternoon, nearly dusk. Suddenly, a very bright light shone through the car window all over me. It was not like any light I had ever seen. I felt so elated I said, 'God, oh God, this must be You. I'll do whatever You tell me to do.'

"But after the light left, I was no longer elated. Instead I felt sad and guilty with the life I'd been living. It was as if God was pointing me to a better way. I made a decision to deal with the wrong things in me, to learn from all the bad that had happened and to build a new future."

Then the mother wrote me this: "I checked out the time when you and the woman who used to be an alcoholic began to pray. It was just before Sandra felt the light of God's presence. What timing!"

This was the beginning of Sandra's transformation. Her mother reported that she slowly emerged from her social paralysis. She attended a nurse's reunion. She's looking for a new job. We continue to pray for Sandra.

This kind of praying does add up to a super natural kind of protection. The super element is prayer that enters into spiritual warfare with the Enemy who seeks our destruction any way he can get it. Not enough of God's people realize that a heavenly host of protection is available to us if we but call for them.

Catherine and Leonard LeSourd have learned about this protective power. Since they have reported some of my experiences through their publications (Catherine in *Guideposts* and *The Intercessors*, Len through Chosen Books), it's my turn now to relate a never-before-told story that happened to their family.

Catherine and Len get up early each morning to meditate and pray together. Many of their concerns involve protection, especially for the members of their family who travel so extensively. Over the years they have prayed the prayer of protection so often that Len has developed it visually

"When my son would be driving home from college in wintry weather," Len told me, "I saw in my spirit a protecting angel sitting on the left front hood of his car, ready to ward off danger. I believe that there is a vast host of angelic forces available to us when we call for help and protection in the name of Jesus."

When his daughter, Linda, and new husband, Phil Lader, flew to Israel recently, Len visualized a small force of angels guarding their plane as it flew through the strife-torn Middle East air lanes, and also protecting the cars and buses they used in sightseeing.

The LeSourds' most harrowing experience occurred some twelve years ago, when their sons Chet and Jeff were teenagers. Len, Catherine and the two boys were driving from the north to their home in Boynton Beach, Florida. The morning before they started, Len asked for spiritual protection as he always did on such trips.

The trip was made without incident. The LeSourds arrived at their home on a scorchingly hot, September afternoon. After unpacking the car, the two boys seemed about to jump into the pool for a swim as they usually did. Instead they went to their rooms to relax and Len began checking things around the house.

When dusk came, he started to turn on the light switch which was located underwater in their small swimming pool. The light always created a very beautiful glow on their patio. But Len made a disturbing discovery. The pool light switch was already in the "on" position. Obviously the light had burned out.

Or — and then a prickly feeling crept through his body. Could the light have shorted out from the water somehow? If so, the pool water could be dangerously electrified.

Quickly he put the switch in the "off" position and taped it over, warning the rest of the family not to touch it. Len then reviewed what he knew about pool lights. Special legislation had been passed several years before, ruling out pool lights underwater unless they were enclosed in a special water-tight unit that guaranteed their being leak-proof. But nothing could be done about pool lights installed before this legislation was passed unless individual pool owners took the necessary action. Len had no idea what kind of pool light had been installed in their pool because they had purchased their home from another couple several years after it had been built.

An electrician was called. He came, checked the pool light carefully, then summoned Len with a very sober look on his face.

"How long had the switch been in the 'on' position?"

"I don't know."

"Nobody went swimming, obviously."

"Not that I know of."

"T'would have been too bad if they had."

"You mean the pool was electrified?"

"Had to be. Water leaked into the light socket and shorted out the circuit. The current then soaked the pool water. We've had too many deaths from this sort of thing. I've disconnected the circuit. Don't ever try and reconnect it without getting a whole new unit.

Len then called his family together and asked his sons why they hadn't plunged into the pool the moment they got home as they ordinarily did.

They looked puzzled. "For some reason we just decided to lie down instead of jumping into the pool," said Chet. "I don't know why."

Len and Catherine certainly knew why.

Later, Len led his family in a prayer of thanksgiving for the Lord's protection, not only during their trip, but especially at an unsuspecting time of deadly danger in their home.

Don't tell Len and Catherine that super natural living isn't very real, or that it doesn't include vast and unseen forces who will come to our aid in times of need or crisis.

10

SUPER NATURAL LOVE

THE URGE TO love and be loved is so strong in all of us. And yet how easy to abuse and misuse this great, natural gift from God.

I watched this happen to Shirley Phillips*, having special concern for her, I guess, because I saw something of me in her — an intense craving for a love that never came as long as she sought it so determinedly.

Aside from that one area, Shirley and I have little in common and we have lived in different sections of the country. Parts of her story are difficult to tell, because for years and years we haven't wanted to look at incest and its ramifications.

It's a long story, too, but one of great hope and encouragement, for it shows in detail how God's love will break through any barrier man erects against Him.

Shirley grew up in a small Vermont community, craving

*All names have been changed.

love from her parents. What she received was inattention from her mother and an attention from her father that seemed very wrong to her. She didn't realize this fully until she was eleven, and even then she wasn't sure that what was happening wasn't somehow her fault.

It was at this point that Shirley's mother confided to her one day this startling news: "Your father is no d--- good."

That was a shocking revelation to Shirley. For she concluded that she couldn't be any good either.

After brooding about this for many days, Shirley came to a decision. At breakfast one morning, she picked up a sharp bread knife and said, "I'm going to kill myself right here at the table."

Her father, mother, and younger brothers and sisters stared at her open-mouthed. But no one moved to try to stop her. Convinced for sure that no one loved her, furious at them all, Shirley threw the knife down and ran to her room, sobbing. From then on she cried a lot alone in her room.

Ed came into her life when she was seventeen. He was a working man, strong, with a temper. She married him to get away from her sexually abusive father. *Now,* she thought, *I'll be loved.*

Two weeks after her marriage, Shirley received her first beating. Ed had been gone all night drinking, and she made the mistake of asking where he had been.

Ed continued to beat Shirley to "keep her in line." When a daughter was born, he began to beat her, too, at the age of nine months. At times he'd haul out a gun, load it up and threaten to shoot his wife if she didn't do what she was told.

Shirley finally reached a point where she would beg Ed to shoot her. Then he'd laugh, throw the gun down and say, "You're crazy!"

A son was born, and Ed doted on him so much it enraged Shirley. When Ed beat their daughter, Shirley retaliated by beating their son. Her idea was, "I won't let him grow up like his father!"

One time, Shirley beat her son with a wire coat hanger till his body was striped with red marks. Though he was only three years old, the boy never even cried. Everyone in the family knew by then that crying didn't change things. In fact, whenever Shirley cried, Ed would beat their daughter even harder.

The day came when Shirley stopped crying. She just held it all inside. Soon, the children learned to do the same. Meanwhile Shirley bore more children, and there were more problems and less money and more fighting.

Finally, Shirley reached a point where she decided the only way to win was to do to her husband exactly what he was doing to her. "If you can't beat them, you might as well join them," she concluded. If he drank, she drank. If he beat her, Shirley would beat back. If he went out, she went out. It was a vicious pattern of sinful living as they played games with their lives and the lives of their children. Since Shirley had grown up without love, she couldn't give love to her husband or five children. Their home was a cesspool of dishonesty, distrust, infidelity, violence and hatred.

Years passed. One day, a stranger entered Shirley's life. She was about forty-five, heavy-set, the mother of a girl who went to school with Shirley's oldest daughter. Shirley did not like Ethel particularly, because she asked questions and made Shirley feel guilty.

One day, Ethel invited Shirley to a Bible study group. Shirley quickly refused. A week later Ethel came to visit and again invited her to attend this study group. Shirley had a vague knowledge of the Bible, but she knew it threatened everything she thought and did. Once again she refused.

It turned out that Ethel was a widow who had to sell cleaning products to make a living. Shirley felt sorry for her and bought a bottle. A month went by and Ethel did not return. Shirley liked the cleaning product so much she finally called Ethel and said she needed another bottle.

"I can't get to your house," Ethel told her. "Could you meet me at the Friendship Center to pick it up?"

"Yes," said Shirley. "Tell me the time and place."

When Shirley hung up the phone, she realized she had been tricked into going to the Bible study.

Somehow she found a Bible, and the next morning headed grimly to Friendship Center where the group met, determined to go there once, get Ethel off her back and pick up her cleaning product. During the meeting, Shirley argued with the leader all the time she was there, and then went again and again, determined to prove to those ladies that they were too far out. The group was studying Galatians and the word "free" kept coming up over and over again. "Free" was what Shirley had always wanted to be. Free from this life, anyway. She had tried to commit suicide several times to be free. She was caught by that word.

One day it happened. As the women prayed for Shirley, a love poured over her. Now she knew that this love was what she had missed and wanted all her life. A love that was not demanding, not corrupted, not manipulative, but pure and unreserved. This was the love of Jesus.

As Jesus loved Shirley, He began to cleanse her of all the filth and anger and guilt that dominated her life. Shirley just couldn't believe there was a love like that. Her body was so starved for it that she couldn't wait until Bible study day arrived. She sought out Ethel and the other women at every opportunity, drinking in their words, hungering for their prayers, yearning for more of this Savior who was so radically changing her life.

Shirley's husband quickly sensed that there was something new in his wife. Ed was a jealous man and squared for a fight. "Tell me who he is," he demanded one night.

"What are you talking about?"

"That guy who makes you act so stupid."

"There's no guy."

"There is. I'm no dummy. You have a silly look in your eyes. Some man's done that."

"Some man!" Shirley threw back her head and laughed. "You're right, Ed. He is some Man."

"I'll kill him."

Shirley stared at her husband. "You can't. He died years ago."

For a moment, it was Ed who looked blank. "You're lying," he finally said.

"Jesus died on the cross nearly 2000 years ago," Shirley continued. "But He came back from the dead. He loves me, Ed. He loves me in a way you never have — or could. He has changed my life."

Ed stared at his wife and struggled with a series of emotions — confusion, jealousy, anger, frustration. Then he stormed out the front door.

Hours later he came back roaring drunk. Shirley was sitting in their living-room chair reading the Bible. When Ed entered, she placed the Bible on the floor beside her chair. The first thing he did was kick the Bible clear across the room.

Then he began slapping Shirley until she fell on the floor, sobbing in pain.

"Let your Jesus help you now," Ed charged as he stomped out.

Shirley was sorely tempted to flee her violent husband and her five children who all had problem personalities. But the new Person in her life wouldn't let her quit. As He loved her, she was going to try and love her family. It would be slow and painful going, but He assured her, *"I will be with you."*

Ed was surly and resistant and confused by his wife's new love. But something significant happened after that one evening when he had come home so drunk. The beatings stopped. Never again did Ed strike his wife.

Shirley began to talk to Ed about her new faith cautiously, but firmly. "God saved me, Ed, and He wants to save you too."

"Save me from what?" Ed would snap.

"Save you from the misery and anger and pain you feel inside yourself."

"How do you know how I feel?"

"Because I felt the same way before Jesus came into my heart and began to love me."

Ed would snort, and tromp off to bed.

Their two youngest children were next after Shirley to receive Jesus as Lord. Shirley began to say a blessing before each meal. Ed couldn't take it. "Why thank God when I bought the food?" he grunted.

From then on in her prayer, Shirley thanked Daddy for the food and God for Daddy. After a few weeks of this Ed asked his wife to shut up about Daddy, to thank God for the food and be done with it.

A year later on New Year's Eve, Ed and Shirley volunteered to babysit for his sister's children while they were away. They took their youngest children with them and were all watching a program put on by Rex Humbard. Ed liked the singing, but was put off when Rex gave the invitation for television watchers to surrender their lives to Jesus.

The children were all for it. "Can we pray too, Daddy?" they asked.

It was one of those unforgettable and suspenseful moments. Ed's face was a study in conflicting emotions. "Sure," he finally said. Then to Shirley's joy and amazement he got down on the floor with them and repeated the words that committed his life to Jesus Christ.

The next day, Ed tried to play it down, and was obviously a bit frightened by his action the night before. When Shirley suggested one day he should tell people on the job what he had done, he said, "Oh, I could never do that." Yet Shirley discovered later that he had talked about Jesus to everyone at work.

When asked to pray with the family, Ed said, "Oh, no.

Never. I can talk to God alone, but I can't pray aloud." But soon he was saying grace, and then praying with the family.

Since Ed never had a formal education, he was poor at reading and knew almost nothing of the Bible. He finally reached out and begged God to let him read the Bible. "Just Your Word, Lord, even if I can't read anything else."

The Holy Spirit then became his Teacher, giving him the ability to read and understand the Bible. He also was given a love for his family. Ed and Shirley never knew what love was until the Lord loved them first.

Attacks from Satan followed. Ed's assaults were over his dead loved ones. He had lost his father, then two brothers in the same car wreck. His mother died. Then while he was drunk, Ed had run over and killed his best friend. Finally, his sister was killed in a car accident. He'd hear their voices in dreams, and they'd torment him. It was so bad he couldn't sleep.

Another obsession was his jealousy over Shirley. It was so intense at times that Ed would hate to leave for his construction job because of an unreasonable fear of what his wife might do while he was away.

One night he had a dream, and in it the Lord asked him, "Do you love Me?"

Ed replied, "Yes, Lord, I really do."

Next the Lord asked, "Does your wife love Me?"

Ed said, "Oh yes, does she ever!"

The Lord then told him, "Well, Ed, if she loves Me, you can trust her because I won't let her do the things you think she does."

Ed's jealousy ended at that point.

Satan began attacking Shirley's past, making her miserable. "I knew I wasn't any good," she told me. "I was ashamed of my sins and would cry a lot during the day and go through my childhood over and over in my mind. Then I would pray, 'Oh Lord, take this part of my life and heal it. It hurts so bad that it's coming between me and Thee." Immediately after the prayer, Shirley would receive peace about that particular stage of her childhood.

One night, she had a dream in which Jesus took her back into her childhood. Here is how she reported it:

> *All night we ran through a meadow and played tag, and finally He sat me down, and I can still remember looking into His eyes. Jesus told me, "Shirley, when you were a child, someone else had control of your life. You do not need to feel ashamed about that, because I love you anyway."*

"I've had peace about my childhood ever since," she continued. "I now feel as good as anyone else. I'm no longer insecure and feel I am the enemy. Satan is the enemy, not me. Jesus loves me. Because He loves me, I can love my children and other people as well."

And because of this visit with Jesus, Shirley was finally able to forgive her father for violating her girlhood, even though he had not changed. "I no longer hate him," she told me. "Although I can't yet say I love him, I pray for him and I've forgiven him."

The story of her five children is incomplete. There has been tragedy and heartache.

Shirley's oldest son, Alan, was heavily into drugs, using speed and LSD. At night he'd roll and toss on the floor above Shirley's bedroom, begging God to let him die. All Shirley could think about was the damage she had done to him as a child. Now she was reaping what she had sown.

The saddest part was now that she had learned to love him, he wouldn't let her. All she could do was pray.

Shirley's oldest daughter, Bonnie, became pregnant and was married at fifteen, then divorced at twenty, with two small daughters to rear. When two nervous breakdowns followed, Shirley kept the girls for a year.

Stephanie, the youngest, was five and had been with

Shirley only a month when she asked, "What is all this God business?" She was having nightmares every night, was terror-stricken by the dark and couldn't sleep alone. Over and over again, Shirley told her how much Jesus loved her. "He will send guardian angels to watch over you, Stephanie. Just ask Him and He will send a big one to sit at the foot of your bed to protect you all night long."

Stephanie prayed for this, and soon began sleeping the night through.

Melody, the other child, has been sickly, in and out of hospitals, but "a blessing to us all with her sweet spirit," says Shirley. The child couldn't talk when she came to her grandmother. Now, "Jesus loves me" and "Praise the Lord" are a part of her vocabulary.

Bonnie accepted the Lord during her recuperation, and Shirley is asking the Lord to break the cycle of sin that has gone on in the family from generation to generation.

Shirley's third child, Craig, was into alcohol. He and a friend stole a pickup and headed for Florida. In heartbreak, Shirley paced the floor, unable to eat, too distraught to commit her second son to the Lord and just trust. She kept saying, "Oh Lord, what are You doing? Both sons are in bad trouble! I want *You* to catch them, not the authorities."

The thieves were caught and returned to face charges. Shirley's son was placed on probation.

Shirley summed it up this way: "Well, the Lord and I struggled, and I finally knew I could not live my children's lives for them. Since I could do nothing of myself, I began to pray for my children to be healed inside of the damage I had done them. The Lord moves in mysterious ways. All I know is that He loves me, He loves Ed and He loves every one of my children."

The healing continued. Alan was sentenced to prison where he accepted the Lord. Now her oldest son is witnessing so strongly in prison that a Bible study program was started and fellow prisoners have become believers.

Craig was sent to a training school for boys, joined Alcoholics Anonymous and also committed his life to God.

The youngest two children have not been in trouble, and bring joy to their parents. Shirley praises God for them and for the changes that have taken place in the lives of her husband, children and grandchildren. Quietly, lovingly, persistently, she prays for continued healing in her family, realizing now that it is a lifetime work to restore health to people who spent too many years in moral filth, degradation, and spiritual poverty.

Each day, Shirley rejoices in the miracles that have already taken place through the love of Jesus. That He could love her despite her once despicable condition always amazes her, for she felt she was the lowest of the low. But then the lowest ones often are the quickest to receive Him.

I've learned quite a lot from Shirley's story. God's miracles in people usually take time. He comes into their lives slowly and the changes come slowly. To be sure, there can be moments of sudden illumination, brilliant light, visions and other miraculous phenomena. But He does not often suspend natural laws. He works through them. When we ask Him, He enters our natural state quietly, bringing light to darkness, hope to despair, courage to timidity, vitality to weakness, knowledge to confusion, faith to fear, love to hate. Sometimes we're hardly aware of the change that is taking place in us. On other occasions, the change is obvious, like walking from the cold into a warm room.

God specializes in reaching down to those who struggle with the most natural of human sins, bringing to them His love — a super love because it comes from God. We've all seen it happen many times, yet it is always a new and exciting event when He touches that which is so natural in people, producing a spiritual chemical reaction inside them, which changes and heals and transforms the ordinary into the extraordinary.

11

CREATIVE AGING

MY SEARCH FOR knowledge about super natural living brought me to a group of some sixty million people who live in the United States. The elderly. How do they become what God wants them to be?

Let's take a look at two great-grandmothers in their nineties I happen to know who have birthdays a month apart. One is barely able to walk, has fading eyesight, but her mind is so alive and vital that she conducts a Bible study every Tuesday morning throughout the year.

The other is also crippled in body, has fading eyesight and a mind that functions much like a six-year-old girl. It is pathetic to see her react to almost everything in a child-like way.

There is a medical explanation for the difference between these two women, but I'm not satisfied that it explains fully why some people seem to get more creative and wise as they age, while others grow senile. What makes the difference?

To find the answer, I've read a lot of books and talked to

many elderly people in recent months. The most helpful senior citizen perhaps was the one closest to me.

My father, Glenn Perkins, is now seventy-five. As I write this, he enjoys wonderful health, and is vibrant with the joy of living. When people ask him the secret he tells them, "Years ago I gave God the title to my body. So now it's His obligation and expense to keep up the repairs on it."

He's always looking for another exciting challenge, or one more mountain to climb.

Right after Mother died in 1973, he took his grieving heart to a comfortable place in Florida on a peaceful river. After three months, he was totally bored with retirement and began to pray, "Lord, give me something worthwhile to do."

One day as he was reading his Bible, he came upon this message: "Let your light so shine before *men*, that they may see your good works, and glorify your Father in Heaven" (Matthew 5:16). The word "men" seemed to jump out at him. What did it mean?

Then he turned to Romans 8 and read: "The Spirit helps us in our weakness; for we do not know how to pray as we ought, but the Spirit Himself intercedes for us with sighs too deep for words. And He who searches the hearts of *men* knows what is in the mind of the spirit . . ." (verses 26 & 27, RSV).

Once again the word "men" seemed significant. My father waited and trusted that the Lord would act. A few days later, my brother Jim called him. "Daddy, I know you're settled in a lovely fishing spot on the river, but I've just bought a ranch north of Houston. I need you, not so much for the work but to oversee and look after the *men*, the personnel, the hired hands."

When the word "men" was emphasized, my father knew this was his call from the Lord. Then the first Sunday after he moved to Texas, he attended church. The pastor greeted him with excitement, combined with relief. They needed a teacher of the men's Bible class. My dad had all the qualifications.

And so my father began a new life in his seventies, influencing men in this Texas community. Being sensitive to the Holy Spirit at work inside him kept Dad from going placid in his old age, kept him open to God's guidance, kept alive the creative juices inside him.

The last time I visited him, he told me, "When you're through changing, you're through. A person is insensible to fatigue when he marches to the music of the Spirit. I chose a long time ago to be *permanently* cheerful because of my permanent arrangement with a permanent triumph in Jesus Christ!"

A year or two ago, Dad and five ranch hands were trying to move two mean cows into the loading chute. They had successfully loaded one when the one remaining went on a wild, pawing, snorting rampage straight for the six men. The younger men jumped or climbed over the fence. Daddy held his ground, feeling that he could divert the animal into the loading chute. The cow knocked my father down, trampled on his chest and head before the other men could rescue him.

My brother, Jim, told us later that he was paralyzed with fear when they took Daddy to the hospital. "Dad looked awful, lying there so lifeless, so beaten and bruised."

My father remained unconscious for seven long hours. When he revived, his memory was gone. He had always been so witty, so able to bounce back, it was frightening. When the nurses propped him up to try to feed him, he was totally oblivious to what was happening. Then a transformation took place, as if something on the inside clicked on. He bowed his head and asked God's blessing on the food. Then lifting his head, he prayed strongly for himself and for everyone in the hospital including nurses, doctors and visitors. The nurses were amazed that the action was so involuntary. Nor does he remember doing it. The inner candle of the Spirit is not snuffed out easily — it cannot be extinguished or trampled.

I was getting ready to break some engagements and fly to his side when Jim called to say Daddy had been released from the hospital. He had no broken bones, and a clear mind. Several days later, he was straining to go back to work even though his left arm was still in a sling. Within a few weeks, he was driving the tractor again.

There's a super natural quality to this seventy-five-year-old that doctors can't explain. The inner light not only makes his mind sharp, but must emanate a certain kind of ray that keeps his body young. This is the same man who smoked so much at the age of twenty that he was called "medically tubercular." When Dad made his body a temple for the Holy Spirit, the smoking ended and health returned to his lungs.

Dad explains it all very simply today on the basis of Job 22:23. "I return unto the Lord," he says, "and *He builds me up.*"

My grandmother, Mom Perky, was another who had this "forever spring" attitude. She was no natural beauty, but there was a sparkle about her that attracted people she met in the grocery store, on the street and wherever she went. She said it came from her "magic morning" therapy.

Each morning upon arising, she would kneel and pray, "Lord, give my *Your* beauty treatment for today. Fill me with Your energy and love for others. Help me enjoy today."

Then she would wait, knowing that she was in God's presence, confident that He never turns a deaf ear to prayer. She told me that she visualized herself as a candle. Her body was like the tallow of the candle and her spirit or soul was like the wick.

"I asked God daily to light my soul (or wick) and set me aflame with His power, to quicken me, to make me alert. Then I asked Him to fan that flame by breathing upon me — the holy breath of God. And I moved close enough to Him to do it."

My grandmother kept her arthritis under control by a

combination of prayer and the use of nature's provision. For example, every morning before breakfast, she drank a cup of warm water in which she put a spoonful of apple cider vinegar and a spoonful of natural honey.

After she died at ninety-one, I began to adopt her "magic morning" therapy into my everyday routine. For at this period in my life, I was becoming aware of one basic fact. Those who had inner resources to cope with the aging process didn't wait until retirement to develop them. I'm sure the Spirit of God will enter anyone, anytime when invited. But if the mind and body have been abused by food, drink and wrong living for sixty or seventy years, an instant inner transformation is difficult.

So it was that I began a program several years ago, combining the physical and spiritual, as a preparation for the last part of my life.

From Beth Lavender, a writer friend who is fifty-two but looks thirty, I learned of the physical benefits of jumping rope. "For a twenty-nine cent investment, you can have a thin waistline, a firmer bustline, slimmer thighs and a rosy complexion," she told me. "But the doctor advises having a good-fitting bra and not overdoing it during menstruation."

I bought a jump rope, but the prices had already gone up five cents. Beth, an outdoor woman, helped me to combine the natural with the spiritual by an all-day-long prayer attitude. It begins with a time of morning devotions. Then through a deliberate set of her mind, she concentrates on the needs of others throughout the day. The result: little chance for self-pity and self-centeredness, which I've become convinced can drain vitality and speed up the aging process.

In working out my rope-jumping program, I found it zestful to sing faith-building choruses as I exercised. Such as:

Greater Is He that Is in You, Than He that Is in
    the World;
If God Be for Us, Who Can Be Against Us?;

Praise the Name of Jesus;
The Joy of the Lord Is My Strength;
and Wonderful, Wonderful, Jesus Is to Me.

Sometimes I quote Scriptures over and over while jumping the rope to take away the monotony. In the winter, I jump near a window with a view. In the summer, I try to jump somewhere outdoors, sucking in the fresh air.

One day, it came to me that I should sing more, that music so delights the Lord that I need to practice more down here for what will be an important part of heaven.

While getting more involved with music, I became aware of something else. The "rest" or pause in music is important to establish the rhythm. Thus I needed to get plenty of sleep, to rest my mind as well as body. Sunday has now become a day of rest for our family — a time for worship in church and family activities at home.

I walk a mile every day. While I walk briskly, I pray silently. Sometimes I carry a clip board to write down thoughts that come to me. Thoughts come better for me during these times than when I am reclining.

Walking and praying perfectly combine the natural and the spiritual. I enjoy helping my husband cut firewood, love brushing and grooming our horses. Physical work sweeps away the dust of self-centeredness that will gather in my thinking. I can pray while doing these.

My eating habits began changing. I still enjoy meat in small quantities, but I began consuming more and more water, fruit and greens.

I drink peppermint tea, eat mustard greens, dandelion greens, prepared like spinach. I like to drink pumpkin seed tea.

Roman Morris, a well-known health authority, shared with me some of his secrets that can help one to live a long life. Roman is a fine-looking man, a grandfather, who plants and harvests crops on his farm and loves to play tennis. He sums up his philosophy this way: "I breathe deeply, sleep cool, eat sensibly. Early each morning I go outside and, with arms raised high, breathe deeply to get the fresh air down into the lower lobes of my lungs," he explained. "I sleep cool. I'm covered with adequate blankets, but the temperature is cool. And I eat sensibly, always leaving the table before I am completely full. I drink a lot of water to flush out the germs — and rarely have a cold, and never constipation. I take a long walk every day outdoors. I consumer one-half cup of bran each day. I like whole grain cereals and bread. We make our own yogurt for about five cents a cup, and I eat a cup every other day. A good cup of yogurt is equivalent to two penicillin shots.

"I take three brewers' yeast tablets daily for iron, and one seaweed or kelp tablet each day," he continued. "When I first started getting grey, I noticed how black and shiny my stallion was. He always eats the kelp grass at the bottom of the marsh when the water first drains off. I told my doctor this, and he said, 'Yes, it would work for people, but they don't like the taste of kelp. However, the tablets are almost tasteless.' I believe that is why my hair shines and that there is little grey in it.

"I ride a bicycle often in summer, and have an exercise bike in the basement, which I can use in the winter."

The Scripture passage that most challenges Roman: "His flesh shall be fresher than a child's; he shall return to the days of his youth" (Job 33:25).

The turning point in Roman's life came when the Lord helped him stop smoking. "Every time I craved a smoke, I would pray," he said. "Many times, I had to do this in awkward situations — when we had company, or when I was on the tennis court. But it was pray or else. I was desperate to quit. My wife thinks that my praying so often in these public situations forced me to quit or suffer humiliation. I'm convinced that it was God's mercy that finally took away the desire."

G.J. Winter is an energetic, elderly gentlemen who has been ushering at our church for thirty-six years, and he says that his vitality comes from God. During the week, he sells men's clothing, driving close to a thousand miles in five days.

The other day, he said, "It's only January, but I've already sold my spring line. Now I can hardly wait to get in my fall line and go to work on it."

Mr. Winter is ninety-three years old. He has been a salesman for seventy years, still has a quick step, a bright smile and enthusiasm for life. That's super natural living.

In recent months I've pondered the question raised by the two great-grandmothers described at the beginning of this chapter—one so crippled in body and child-like in mind, the other crippled in body but with a mind very alive and vital and faith-charged. Since they were of approximately the same age, what caused the difference in mental outlook?

The research I've done and the people I've talked to have shed much light on the subject: *it is important to prepare physically for one's latter years,* and this involves proper exercise and food. But there is something even more important which I sum up this way.

Our efforts to find the key to longevity and the secret of keeping a sound mind as the body deteriorates lie only partly in our physical preparation and more importantly in the spiritual.

From what I've learned about the two great-grandmothers, there was little difference in their physical life. Both loved to garden. Both were active physically. Neither drank or smoked. Their bodies deteriorated in the same way: eye problems, walking problems and so forth.

The difference was in their spiritual life. Though both were church members, the similarity ends there. The woman who reverted to a child-like mentality in her old age had shunned her inner spirit, whereas the other had sought the

Holy Spirit, absorbed Scripture daily and opened up every part of her life to the Lord in prayer.

I'm hesitant to draw any final conclusions on this subject, for much more research should be done. But all that I've learned and experienced so far leads me to this passage which points the direction for us all:

"Do you not know that your body is a temple of the Holy Spirit within you which you have from God? You are not your own; you were bought with a price. So glorify God in your body" (I Corinthians 6:19-20, RSV).

Of one thing we can be sure — super natural living can last all the years of our life.

12

TO THE NEXT LIFE

JUST AS GOD gives us the tools for super natural living on His earth, He points us toward the high road to take when we leave this world.

To put it another way, a man leaves this world in the same fashion that he has lived in it.

You may say, "That's just your opinion, Betty. You have no proof. No one knows what death will bring us."

That's true. But we are learning more and more about death and the life thereafter. The evidence is accumulating in a variety of ways.

Several years ago I was in Los Angeles, appearing on a television program where I described my own experience of being clinically dead. I was hardly back in my hotel room when the telephone rang. The caller identified himself as a news photographer.

"I watched the program tonight where you described the way you died and then returned to life," he said. "I had that experience, too. I was riding my motorcycle to the scene of a forest fire when another car hit me broadside. In the ambulance I died and fell into a fiery cave. It was horrible. There was no lovely light or beautiful music. The medical man in the back of the ambulance got my heart to beating just before I hit the bottom of that fiery cave. I came back to this world screaming and shaking. Now I am in real trouble at night, for when I start to fall asleep, I fall into that same fiery cave. I have the same nightmare over and over again. Now, Mrs. Malz, one of us is lying about death since we certainly didn't see the same thing or go to the same place."

"Neither of us has lied," I replied. "I believe we were just heading in different directions toward opposite destinies. Do you believe in God?"

"I don't want to talk about religion," he cut me off.

"I believe God loves you very much to give you a second chance at life. He is telling you to change the course you are now traveling or you will spend eternity in that fiery cave . . ."

There was a click at the other end. He had hung up the phone.

Minutes later, he called back and apologized, saying he didn't like being preached at. I could have tried to relate to him with a few bland statements. Instead, I found myself stating to him that we have the promise of eternal life through Jesus Christ. Then I read him this passage in the Book of Revelation: "And whosoever was not found recorded in the Book of Life, was cast into the lake of fire" (Rev. 20:15).

He still wanted to argue, but finally agreed to locate a Bible and look up some of the passages I gave him. Then I prayed with him over the phone.

Appearing with me on this same television program was Dr. Maurice Rawlings, a heart specialist in Chattanooga, Tennessee. He has done some astonishing documentation*

---

*Beyond Death's Door, Maurice Rawlings; published by Thomas Nelson Publishing, Ltd., Nashville, TN.

of patients who have died and then through resuscitation been brought back to life. When we presented our findings to television viewers, I would tell my story first, then Dr. Rawlings would describe from the medical point of view what he had learned after interviewing those clinically dead patients who were returned to life.

The doctor had records of about 300 cases. Of these, approximately eighty percent had a horrible experience like that of the news photographer. Only twenty percent had a peaceful experience similar to mine, where they saw Jesus in beautiful light, heard lovely music and felt a kind of ecstasy.

Dr. Rawlings' description of one case held even the television technicians in rapt attention. The patient was a forty-eight-year-old, rural mail carrier with an attractive personality. While in the doctor's office taking a stress test, he crumpled to the floor, lifeless. Dr. Rawlings immediately started an external heart massage while one of the nurses initiated mouth-to-mouth breathing.

The patient revived, opened his eyes and screamed, "I'm in hell!" Then he lost consciousness, stopped breathing and died once more. They reapplied resuscitation methods. Once again the patient revived and screamed, "I'm in hell!"

Usually, the first thing a patient says to Dr. Rawlings after being resuscitated is, "Take your hands off my chest. You're hurting me." In this case, however, the revived man pleaded, "Don't stop!" There was terror on his face. In fact, the patient was perspiring and trembling so violently, he looked as if his hair was "on end."

"Don't you understand," he finally shouted. "I'm in hell. Don't let me go back there." Then he said something which further startled the doctor, "Pray for me."

Dr. Rawlings told him he was a doctor not a preacher, but the man was so desperate the doctor stumbled through a prayer which he had the patient repeat after him. The man's condition then stabilized. That night the doctor went home, dusted off his Bible and tried to find the passages in it where hell was mentioned. Weeks later he had become so involved in the Bible that he committed his life to Jesus and began to write a book about death.

The doctor's follow-up with the rural mail carrier was to go see the man in his hospital room and ask him some questions about what he had seen in hell. The patient could remember nothing! Apparently the experience was so frightening and painful that his conscious mind could not cope with it and so had blotted it out. However, Dr. Rawlings stayed in contact with his patient, and learned that right after his hospitalization the man became an active believer and dedicated church-goer.

After appearing in a half-dozen shows together, Dr. Rawlings and I concluded that the growing number of these experiences confirm the biblical statement, "Strait is the gate, and narrow is the way, which leadeth unto life, and few there be that find it" (Matthew 7:14).

I firmly believe that God permits these experiences to happen to us at the doorway to the next world to affirm the fact that His promises in Scripture are rock solid. With the natural mind we could not grasp or comprehend the whole truth about heaven, but more and more He gives us glimpses.

We had such a glimpse through my uncle, Jess Mullins. Uncle Jess lived all-out, whether it was running a business or leading the congregational singing in his church. He did not have a trained voice, but he did have a personality that induced people to worship and sing with heart — and volume.

After a two-year struggle with cancer, during which time he fought against death with every ounce of determination he possessed, his last moments came in a hospital room. Standing close by were his wife, Aunt Gertrude, their son, Ken, and daughter, Debi. They grieved while they witnessed his suffering and watched his vitality wane. But Uncle Jess had no intention of leaving with a whimper.

One of the songs he most loved to lead was "Jesus is the Joy of Living." As the end neared his face became radiant. Rising up in his bed, he was once again directing the singing in church. Over and over he sang, "Jesus is the Joy of Living" until the breath left his body. He could just as well have been singing, *Jesus is the joy of leaving.*

The beauty and joy of my uncle's death reminded me of this poem*:

> Death's bonds are just a tangled rope
> Which has a child caught in its web.
> Vainly struggling the trapped child weeps.
> Hearing the frightened, hopeless cry,
> His Father leans down, tugs gently,
> And frees His beloved from death's hold.
> With a joyful, thankful cry of rapture,
> The child leaps to his Father's arms.

My growing research includes this story told me by two Catholic sisters, both registered nurses, who worked at St. Bernard's Hospital in Milbank, South Dakota. One was attending a two-year-old boy who had developed pneumonia. While the doctors were doing an emergency tracheotomy, the boy's heart stopped beating.

A frantic series of massages got the heart pumping again. When the little lad opened his eyes and started moving his lips, one of the nurses placed her finger over the hole in his neck so he could speak. Looking at his mother and daddy, he said, "Jesus loves me."

"Who told you that?" asked his father.

"He did. He told me. I saw Him!" the child excitedly reported.

The young parents were stunned. Since they did not attend church, had never discussed religion, nor read to him from the Bible, how could he know anything about Jesus — unless he had really *met* Him during the crisis on the operating table?

For the thousandth time, it brought back my own

*by Sharon Perkins

encounter with Jesus. There was my "death" in the Terre Haute Hospital after weeks of suffering with peritonitis, then the sudden transfer to beautiful open country, walking on vivid, velvety, green grass, through waving meadows of blooming flowers, beside a tall, silent, robed figure. We came upon a magnificent silver structure. A gate opened and I was dazzled by the light. I saw no figure yet was conscious of a Person. And then I knew that the Light was Jesus and the Person was Jesus.

My body had begun to glow, every part of me absorbing the Light. I felt bathed by the rays of a powerful, penetrating loving energy. I seemed to have a choice — to go inside with Him or to go back. I had longed with all my being to go inside, but it didn't seem the right time.

When I returned to my hospital bed and opened my eyes, a direct ray of light was coming through the window. On the beam was emblazoned the words of Jesus, "I am the resurrection and the life: he that believeth in me, though he were dead, yet shall he live" (John 11:25). As I reached out to touch the light and the words, I knew that I had not only come back from the world beyond, but that my body was healed.

Still lingering in my consciousness, years after this experience, is the reality of it. In some ways heaven was more real then the endless procession of days I've lived through in this world since. I can still feel that soft grass and see those awesomely vivid colors and that light.

Another word to describe it is *natural*, for God loves to work through the natural, giving us in the process a peek into His *super* realm. It's as if the root of everything we call natural in this world stems from His place. For heaven, to me, is now a place — a specific location. The heavenly city is every good and natural thing we like in our own cities developed to the highest degree: beautiful buildings, the brightness of carefully groomed parks, the rhythmical hum of machines, the happy shouts of children at play and, over all, the sound of music. And what music! Singing in eight-part harmony, melodious beyond anything we can imagine.

Perhaps you can understand now why this experience has changed my whole approach to death. Any fear of it is completely gone, for I have met that glorious Person at the door and been bathed in the indescribable splendor surrounding Him. When the time comes for me to go through that door, I will do so with great eagerness.

I trust Jesus completely. Didn't He tell us that "in my Father's house are many mansions; if it were not so, I would have told you. I go to prepare a place for you . . . and receive you unto myself; that where I am, there ye may be also" (John 14:2-3).

And so, as I learn to live here and now in a super natural way, I can look forward to the super natural when it's time to leave this world.

Where is heaven?

None of us knows for sure, of course, but I'm convinced that it is a place like England or America — yet vast and glorious beyond our comprehension. The God who created this marvelous world and millions of other planets would also create a heaven of incomparable splendor and magnificence, especially since it is His home.

It will have more than beauty; it will produce complete satisfaction and fulfillment for every soul who enters there.

Believing this so strongly, I was thrilled to learn recently that astronomers have discovered a great empty space in the north — in the nebula of the constellation of Orion — a heavenly cavern so gigantic that the mind of man cannot comprehend it, and so brilliantly beautiful that words cannot adequately describe it. These revelations were made possible by gigantic lenses, plus long exposures of photographic plates, which in turn can be further magnified. This increases the vision of man so tremendously that he is able to peer into the depths of interstellar space and glimpse the vastness of infinity itself. As I read about this, I thought how closely all this confirms the words of Job: "He stretcheth out the north over the empty place" (Job 26:7).

Astronomers seem to agree that there is a huge opening in Orion which is perhaps more than sixteen trillion miles in diameter. This means that across the entrance of this opening in the north, there could be 30,000 solar systems like ours with a sun in the middle of each — and still there would be room to spare.

One scientist, Mr. Learkin of Mt. Lowe Observatory, describes it this way: "The interior of the cavern is so stupendous that our entire solar system would be lost therein. I have watched it since the days of youth in many telescopes of many powers," he said, "but I never dreamed that the central region is the mouth of a colossal cave. The pen of a writer and the brush of an artist would be lifeless and inert in any attempt to describe this interior; for the depth of the Orion nebula appears like torn and twisted objects and river masses of shining glass, irregular pillars, columns of stalactites in glittering splendor and stalagmites from the mighty floor. The appearance is like that of light shining and glowing behind the clear walls of ivory and pearl, studded with millions of diamonds like shining stars."

The scientist went on to say that there must be some reason why all this grandeur is lavished on this one spot in the heavens. "The colors are a hue peculiar to the Orion and studded around the opening so that they appear as a pavement of starry sand. No wonder the astronomers (many of them not religious), say they feel as if they were in some Almighty 'Presence' while scanning this part of the heavens and become speechless before this great outburst of grandeur extending for trillions of miles through space."

The north seems to have deep significance in God's Word. Psalm 48 begins, "Great is the Lord, and greatly to be praised in the city of our God, in the mountain of His holiness. Beautiful for situation, the joy of the whole earth, is mount Zion, on the sides of the north, the city of the great King" (verses 1-2).

I join with some theological thinking that heaven is another era, a middle dispensation in the eternal plan. While we are enjoying heaven, God will purge the earth with fire, and recreate it without sin, sickness or competition from sinful men. After that, we shall return to earth again. We shall inherit the earth. Those who were faithful and overcame sin and temptation here on earth, will rule as kings, queens and priests eternally over kingdoms set up later. Our victories here on earth will be the testing ground for our worthiness to be rulers with Him in the millennial kingdom.

My glimpse of heaven and convictions about it certainly make me no more authority on "the life beyond" than the thousands of others who have been permitted a tiny look. We are tantalized by such encounters, dissect them in every way we can, and speculate endlessly on heaven and hell.

After doing all this, we always return to the rock solid promises and assurances in Scripture about eternal life:

> "Eye hath not seen, nor ear heard, neither have entered into the heart of man, the things which God hath prepared for them that love him" (I Corinthians 2:9).

> "To him that overcometh will I grant to sit with me in my throne, even as I also overcame, and am set down with my Father in his throne" (Revelation 3:21).

> "The hour is coming ... when the dead shall hear the voice of the Son of God: and they that hear shall live" (John 5:25).

> "And this is the will of him that sent me, that everyone which seeth the Son, and believeth on him, may have everlasting life: and I will raise him up at the last day" (John 6:40).

"Jesus said unto her, 'I am the resurrection, and the life: he that believeth in me, though he were dead, yet shall he live" (John 11:25).

"Be ye therefore ready also: for the Son of man cometh at an hour when ye think not" (Luke 12:40).

"For God so loved the world, that he gave his only begotten Son, that whosoever believeth in him should not perish, but have everlasting life" (John 3:16).